China Briefing

The Practical Application of China Business

AF810792

For further volumes:
http://www.springer.com/series/8839
http://www.asiabriefingmedia.com

Dezan Shira & Associates is a specialist foreign direct investment practice, providing business advisory, tax, accounting, payroll and due diligence services to multinationals investing in China, Hong Kong, India and Vietnam. Established in 1992, the firm is a leading regional practice in Asia with nineteen offices in four jurisdictions, employing over 170 business advisory and tax professionals.

We also provide useful business information through our media and publishing house, Asia Briefing

Dezan Shira & Associates
Chris Devonshire-Ellis
Samantha L. Jones · Eunice Ku
Editors

The Yangtze River Delta

Business Guide to the Shanghai Region

Fifth Edition

Springer DEZAN SHIRA & ASSOCIATES

Editors
Dezan Shira & Associates
Kowloon
Hong Kong SAR

Chris Devonshire-Ellis
Dezan Shira & Associates
Asia Briefing Ltd.
132 Nathan Road
Tsim Sha Tsui, Unit 1618
16/F., Miramar Tower
Kowloon, Hong Kong SAR

Samantha L. Jones
Dezan Shira & Associates
Asia Briefing Ltd.
132 Nathan Road
Tsim Sha Tsui, Unit 1618
16/F., Miramar Tower
Kowloon, Hong Kong SAR

Eunice Ku
Dezan Shira & Associates
Asia Briefing Ltd.
132 Nathan Road
Tsim Sha Tsui, Unit 1618
16/F., Miramar Tower
Kowloon, Hong Kong SAR

ISSN 2191-0634 ISSN 2191-0642 (electronic)
ISBN 978-3-642-27623-1 ISBN 978-3-642-27624-8 (eBook)
DOI 10.1007/978-3-642-27624-8
Springer Heidelberg New York Dordrecht London

Library of Congress Control Number: 2012936108

© Asia Briefing Ltd. 2008, 2011, 2012
This work is subject to copyright. All rights are reserved by the Publisher, whether the whole or part of the material is concerned, specifically the rights of translation, reprinting, reuse of illustrations, recitation, broadcasting, reproduction on microfilms or in any other physical way, and transmission or information storage and retrieval, electronic adaptation, computer software, or by similar or dissimilar methodology now known or hereafter developed. Exempted from this legal reservation are brief excerpts in connection with reviews or scholarly analysis or material supplied specifically for the purpose of being entered and executed on a computer system, for exclusive use by the purchaser of the work. Duplication of this publication or parts thereof is permitted only under the provisions of the Copyright Law of the Publisher's location, in its current version, and permission for use must always be obtained from Springer. Permissions for use may be obtained through RightsLink at the Copyright Clearance Center. Violations are liable to prosecution under the respective Copyright Law.
The use of general descriptive names, registered names, trademarks, service marks, etc. in this publication does not imply, even in the absence of a specific statement, that such names are exempt from the relevant protective laws and regulations and therefore free for general use.
While the advice and information in this book are believed to be true and accurate at the date of publication, neither the authors nor the editors nor the publisher can accept any legal responsibility for any errors or omissions that may be made. The publisher makes no warranty, express or implied, with respect to the material contained herein.

Printed on acid-free paper

Springer is part of Springer Science+Business Media (www.springer.com)

About Asia Briefing's China Business Guides

Thank you for buying this guide. China Briefing's publications are designed to fill a niche in the provision of information about business in China.

When we decided several years ago to commence this series, we did so with the knowledge that much information about China is scattered, contradictory, expensive or available only in Chinese. This guide is designed to change that and pull together the practical information you need for doing business in China in an accessible and engaging form.

The articles and materials within have been researched and written in China by those familiar with the issues faced by foreign invested enterprises. To compile this guide, we have engaged the assistance of a respected professional services firm: Dezan Shira & Associates. Without this firm's assistance this book would not have been possible, and we wholeheartedly recommend their services.

Contributors, editors and designers of previous editions of this guide include: Lucy Brady, Edward Boyle, Chua Siew Joo, Robert Deng, Chris Devonshire-Ellis, Rosario Di Maggio, Marco Ferrari, Daniel Hughes, Becky Jian, Charles Racine, Edward Robinson, Joyce Roque, Andy Scott, Graham Thompson, Nazia Vasi, Natalie Wirska, Sam Woollard, Jennifer Wu, Jeffy Yuan, Vicky Zhang.

Contributors to the current edition include: Julia Gu, Eunice Ku, Simon Sheung, Kaitlin Shung, Lena Xia. This edition was designed by Chris Wei and edited by Samantha L. Jones.

At China Briefing, our motto is "the practical application of China business" and we hope that within this volume and our other publications you feel that we have achieved this. Sincerely, Asia Briefing.

Sincerely,
Asia Briefing

Contents

1 **Setting the Scene** 1
The China Picture 1
Shanghai & the YRD
in Perspective 10

2 **Provinces and Cities of the YRD** . . . 17
Shanghai 17
Jiangsu Province 24
Changzhou 30
Nanjing 35
Suzhou 40
Changshu 45
Kunshan 48
Taicang 51
Wuxi 54
Yangzhou 59
Zhejiang Province 64
Hangzhou 71
Ningbo 76
Wenzhou 81
Anhui Province 86
Hefei 93

3 **Establishing Business** 99
Setting up in China 99
Business Taxes 107
Development Zones 111

Appendix, Directory, References 123

Glossary 129

Chapter 1
Setting the Scene

A Socialist Country?

China's market is described as "socialism with capitalist characteristics," wherein the free market largely reins, but the government plays a prominent role and the previously dominant state-owned enterprises (SOEs) still exist in vital sectors. A far cry from its socialist history, Chinese leadership today seems to follow the maxim "to grow rich is glorious."

Dezan Shira & Associates et al. (eds.), *The Yangtze River Delta*, China Briefing, DOI: 10.1007/978-3-642-27624-8_1, © Asia Briefing Ltd. 2012

Deng Xiaoping initiated an "open door policy" in 1978 to reform and modernize the Chinese economy, promoting foreign trade and investment as potential catalysts for growth. In the 30-plus years following reform and opening-up, China's economy developed at an unprecedented rate, averaging about 10% per annum, and that momentum has held steady into the twenty-first century.

1.1 A Changing FDI Identity

China has been the second largest recipient of inward forward direct investment (FDI) in the world, behind the United States, for over a decade. With the assistance of large quantities of FDI, China became the world's factory, but this is now an identity in transition.

Wage rates in China are rising at around 9–15% annually, though increases are higher in coastal cities, such as Beijing, which increased 20% year-on-year in 2010. Further, the increasingly specific, increasingly strong labor legislation is improving worker's rights in China. As such, Southeast Asian countries are increasingly coming to the table as "China alternatives" for labor-intensive manufacturing.

No longer merely a manufacturing haven, China is forging a new identity to present to foreign investors. One aspect of this is the Chinese consumer. The Global Financial Crisis in 2008 had caused an economic downturn in many economies around the world, yet it did virtually nothing to curb China's growing retail sales, which were estimated to have steadily increased by at least 11% year-on-year since 2007. With sales sagging abroad, a variety of foreign firms are investing in China to sell to the Chinese consumer market.

The Chinese government is continually making efforts to encourage foreign investment on its own terms. In 2011, the government announced its 12th Five-Year Plan, which lays the foundations for the economy in the years to come (2011–2016), along with draft revisions to its Foreign Investment Catalogue, which provides industry-specific guidelines on foreign investment utilization. Priority areas for foreign investment under the 12th Five-Year Plan are agriculture, high-tech and green industries.

1.2 A Continent of a Country

China is an incredibly heterogeneous country with vast geographic variations in language, people, industrial specialty and development level. While the wealthiest cities in the country can give European cities a run for their money in terms of modernity, driving a few hours into the countryside will reveal that China is still, in fact, a developing country.

From an administrative perspective, China is divided into municipalities, provinces, autonomous regions and special administrative regions.

China watchers joke that there are so many geographic differences that the country is, in fact, a continent. There are many ways to divide China into more manageable pieces based on shared characteristics, but one of the easiest ways is to look at it as five geographic regions.

China's administrative divisions

Category	Name
Municipalities	Beijing, Tianjin, Shanghai, Chongqing
Provinces[a]	Anhui, Fujian, Gansu, Guangdong, Guizhou, Hainan, Hebei, Heilongjiang, Henan, Hubei, Hunan,Jiangsu, Jiangxi, Jilin, Liaoning, Qinghai, Shaanxi, Shandong, Shanxi, Sichuan, Yunnan, Zhejiang
Autonomous regions	Inner Mongolia, Guangxi, Tibet, Ningxia, Xinjiang
Special administrative regions	Hong Kong, Macau

[a] Taiwan is claimed by the People's Republic of China as a province, but is not covered in China Briefing regional guides

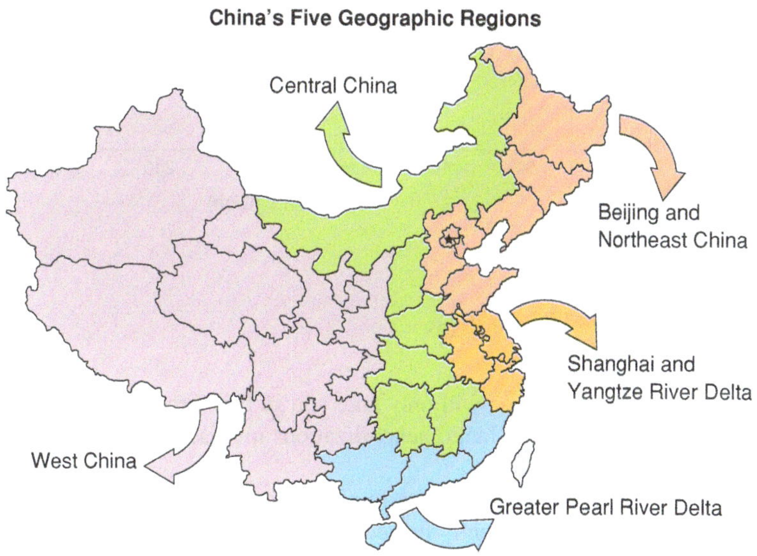

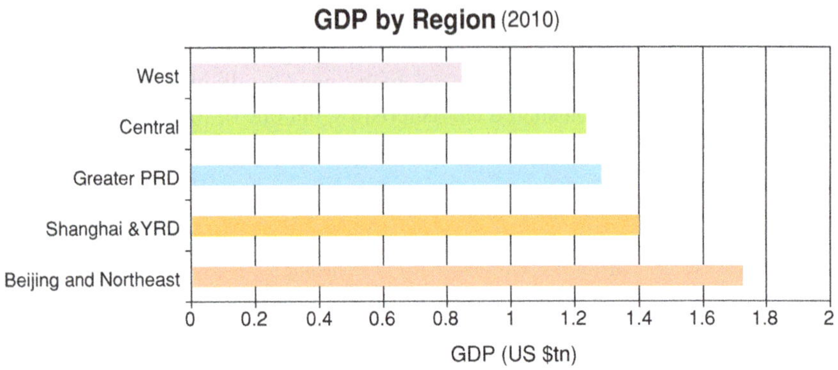

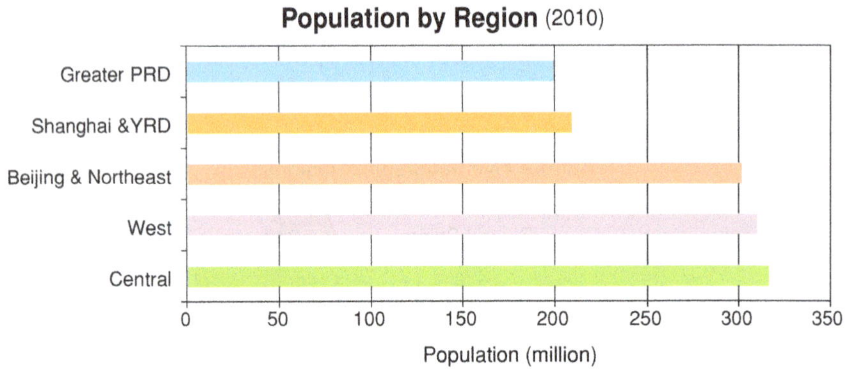

1.3 Beyond First Tier Cities

Looking at provinces in China will only take you so far—broad differences within provinces can make any provincial generalizations misleading. For this reason, in this book we get city-specific.

Cities are often classified according to city tier—first through fourth. The city tier system, while rather inherently flawed in definition, is nonetheless valuable in splitting the Chinese market into more manageable groups.

First tier cities include Beijing, Shanghai, Guangzhou and Shenzhen. Beyond first tier cities, some attempt to define lower city tiers based on population size, while others start with a based definition of provincial capitals and adding and subtracting based on economic indicators. Economic growth, land area, and even high grade transportation facilities (such as international airports) can influence classification as well.

While definitions are inconsistent, the one point that China foreign investment advisors seem to agree on is that second and third tier cities are key to the future of foreign investment in China.

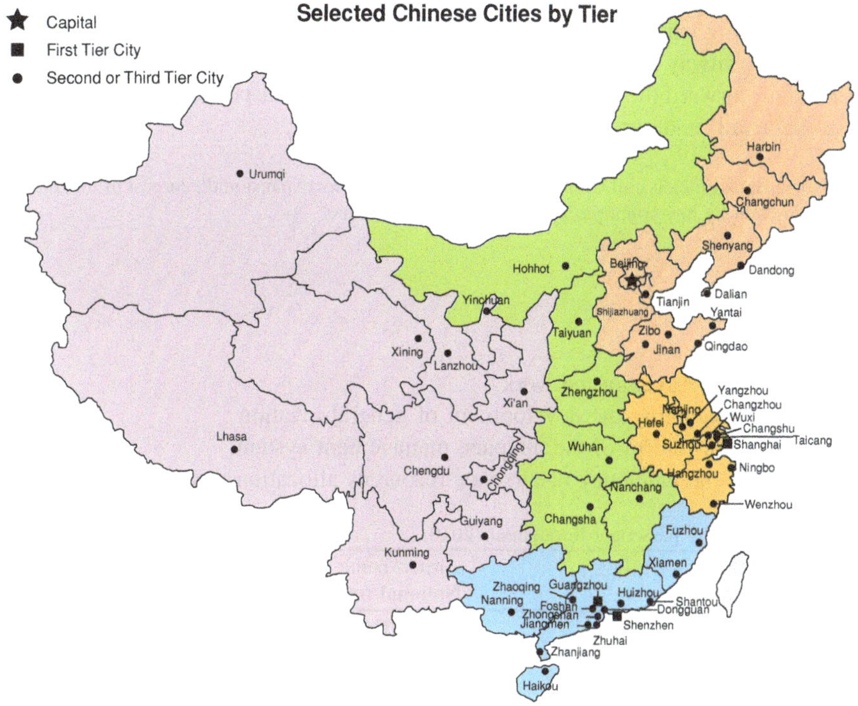

1.4 Infrastructure

China's 12th Five-Year Plan (2011–2015) emphasizes the development of a "comprehensive transportation system." Detailed steps include:

1.4.1 Road

- Improving the planning of the national road network
- Accelerating the construction of roads in the national highway network that are unconstructed or suffer frequent traffic jams
- Reconstruction and expansion of the national and provincial highways
- Completing the construction of the inter-city transportation networks in three major urban agglomerations, namely Beijing-Tianjin-Hebei, Yangtze Delta, and Pearl River Delta

1.4.2 Railway

- Building high-speed railways
- Strengthening the heavy-haul railway network
- Accelerating the construction of passenger-dedicated railway lines, main regional railway lines, and coal transport channels
- Pushing forward the construction of urban railway transportation networks such as light rail, underground rail, and trams

World Bank officials call China's current national railway expansion the largest of its kind undertaken by any country since the nineteenth century.

1.4.3 Air

- Improving the aviation network
- Actively promoting the development of general aviation
- Carrying out reform of the airspace management system
- Increasing the efficiency of airspace resources allocation and utilization

Top 10 Airports by passenger throughput (2010)

National rank	City	Airport name	Passengers (# people)
		National total	**564,312,300**
1	Beijing	Beijing/Capital	73,948,114
2	Guangzhou	Guangzhou/Baiyun	40,975,673
3	Shanghai	Pudong	40,578,621
4	Shanghai	Hongqiao	31,298,812
5	Shenzhen	Shenzhen/Baoan	26,713,610
6	Chengdu	Chengdu/Shuangliu	25,805,815
7	Kunming	Kunming/Wujiaba	20,192,243
8	Xi'an	Xi'an/Xianyang	18,010,405
9	Hangzhou	Xiaoshan	17,068,585
10	Chongqing	Chongqing/Jiangbei	15,802,334

Source National airport throughput rankings, Civil Aviation Administration of China, March 2011

1.4.4 Ports and Waterways

- Vigorously pushing forward the construction of high-grade inland waterways such as the Yangtze River
- Promoting the development of standardization of ships used for inland waterway transportation and the expansion of ports
- Improving the transportation systems for coal, petroleum, iron ore, container, etc.
- Promoting the modernization of the port clusters in the coastal regions

Sea ports by goods throughput (2010)

Rank	Region	Province	Port	Goods throughput (100 million tons)
1	Yangtze River Delta	Zhejiang	Ningbo-Zhoushan	6.33
2	Yangtze River Delta	Shanghai	Shanghai	5.63
3	Northeast China	Tianjin	Tianjin	4.13
4	Greater Pearl River Delta	Guangdong	Guangzhou	4.11
5	Northeast China	Shandong	Qingdao	3.5
6	Northeast China	Shandong	Dalian	3.14
7	Northeast China	Hebei	Qinghuangdao	2.63
8	Northeast China	Hebei	Tangshan	3.46
9	Northeast China	Shandong	Rizhao	2.26
10	Northeast China	Liaoning	Yingkou	2.26
11	Greater Pearl River Delta	Guangdong	Shenzhen	2.21
12	Northeast China	Shandong	Yantai	1.5
13	Greater Pearl River Delta	Guangdong	Zhanjiang	1.36
14	Yangtze River Delta	Jiangsu	Lianyungang	1.27
15	Greater Pearl River Delta	Fujian	Xiamen	1.27
16	Greater Pearl River Delta	Guangxi	Beibuwan (Gulf of Tonkin)	1.19

Source Transportation via public waterways development statistical report, Ministry of Transport, April 2011

Sea ports container throughput (2010)

Rank	Region	Province	Port	Container throughput (million TEU)
1	Yangtze River Delta	Shanghai	Shanghai	2906.93
2	Greater Pearl River Delta	Guangdong	Shenzhen	2250.96
3	Yangtze River Delta	Zhejiang	Ningbo–Zhoushan	1314.65
4	Greater Pearl river Delta	Guangdong	Guangzhou	1254.57
5	Northeast China	Shandong	Qingdao	1201.2
6	Northeast China	Tianjin	Tianjin	1008.62
7	Greater Pearl River Delta	Fujian	Xiamen	582.43
8	Northeast China	Shandong	Dalian	526.25
9	Yangtze River Delta	Jiangsu	Lianyungang	387.06
10	Northeast China	Liaoning	Yingkou	333.84
11	Northeast China	Shandong	Yantai	154.12
12	Greater Pearl River Delta	Fujian	Fuzhou	147.05
13	Greater Pearl River Delta	Fujian	Quanzhou	136.95
14	Northeast China	Shandong	Rizhao	106.1

Source Transportation via public waterways development statistical report, Ministry of Transport, April 2011

National High-speed Train System (12th Five Year Plan)

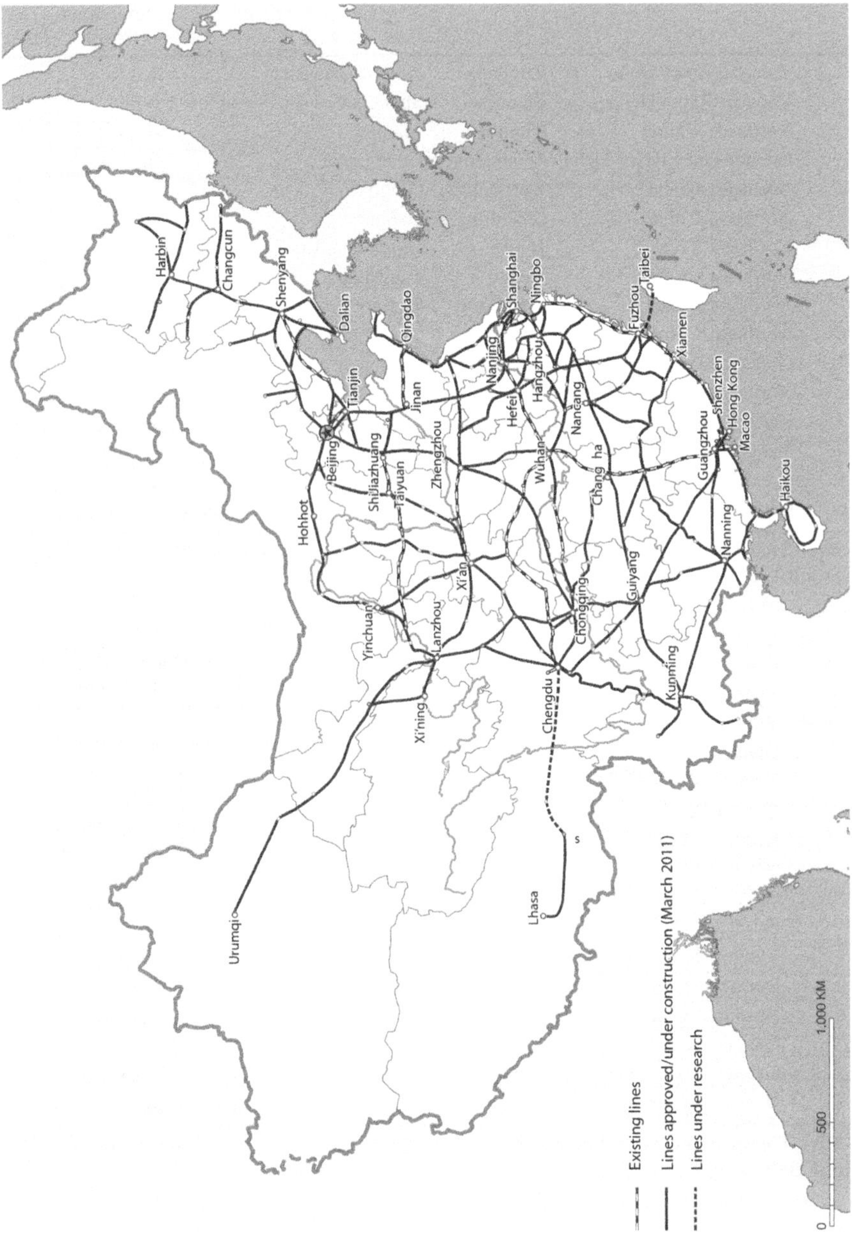

National Expressway System (12th Five Year Plan)

What is the Yangtze River Delta (YRD)?

- Shanghai municipality
- Jiangsu province
- Zhejiang province
- Anhui province

With access to China's largest sea ports, the east coast of China was the first region to develop in China and is the market that most foreign companies consider as their primary entry location for manufacturing. Historically, the YRD has been attractive due to its proximity to suppliers, access to ports, and well-developed infrastructure.

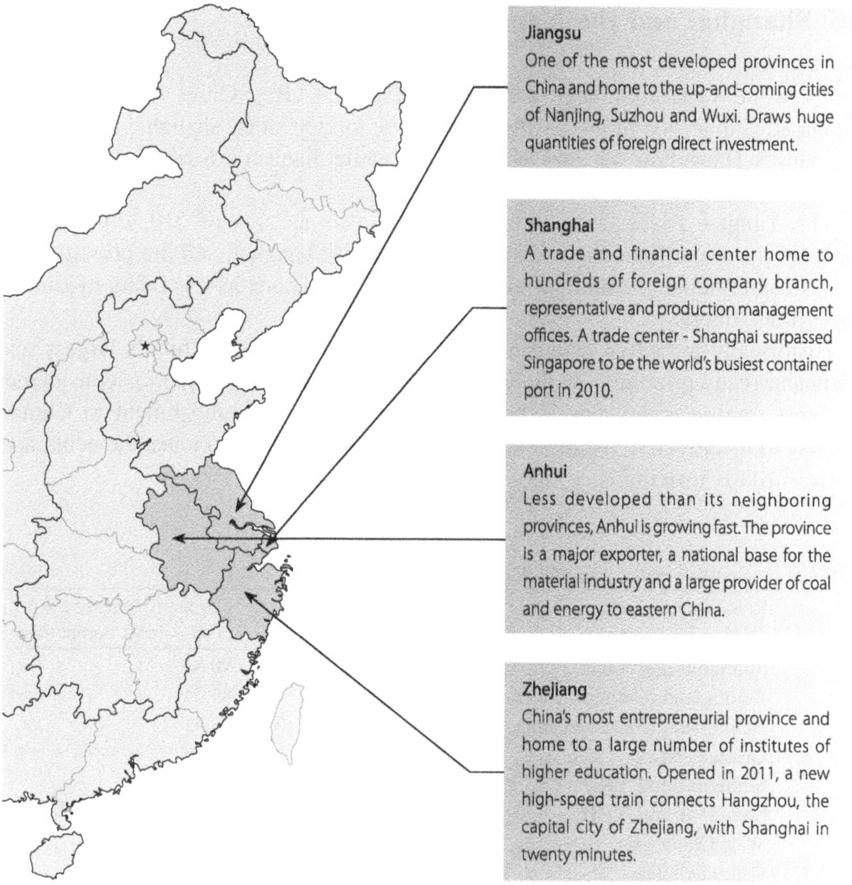
Jiangsu
One of the most developed provinces in China and home to the up-and-coming cities of Nanjing, Suzhou and Wuxi. Draws huge quantities of foreign direct investment.
Shanghai
A trade and financial center home to hundreds of foreign company branch, representative and production management offices. A trade center - Shanghai surpassed Singapore to be the world's busiest container port in 2010.
Anhui
Less developed than its neighboring provinces, Anhui is growing fast. The province is a major exporter, a national base for the material industry and a large provider of coal and energy to eastern China.
Zhejiang
China's most entrepreneurial province and home to a large number of institutes of higher education. Opened in 2011, a new high-speed train connects Hangzhou, the capital city of Zhejiang, with Shanghai in twenty minutes.

1.5 Shanghai and the Yangtze River Delta

Cities in the YRD dominated the Forbes Magazine "Best Cities for Business in Mainland China" list in 2010, filling six of the top ten slots. Shanghai ranked 1st, Zhejiang's Hangzhou 4th and Ningbo 8th, while Jiangsu's Suzhou ranked 5th, Wuxi 7th, and Nanjing 9th.

The Yangtze River Delta (YRD) region covers an area of 210,700 km^2 and includes the major financial and economic hubs of Shanghai, and the provinces of Jiangsu and Zhejiang. Anhui province is also included here, as it is rising to join its eastern neighbors.

Historically attractive to businesses for its easy access to China's largest sea ports and ready proximity to the inland provinces, today this region is considered by most foreign companies to be the primary point of establishment in China. Thanks to its attractive location and supportive government policies, the economy in the YRD is thriving.

National competitive index rankings (2010)

	Region/municipality		Competitiveness ranking (100 = most competitive)
1	**Shanghai and YRD**	**Shanghai**	**90.85**
2	Beijing and Northern China	Beijing	89.31
3	Beijing and Northern China	Tianjin	88.41
4	Greater PRD	Guangdong	87.14
5	**Shanghai and YRD**	**Jiangsu**	**87.13**
6	**Shanghai and YRD**	**Zhejiang**	**85.65**
7	West China	Chongqing	85.49
8	Central China	Hunan	85.4
9	Beijing and Northern China	Shandong	84.41
10	Greater PRD	Fujian	83.93
11	Central China	Hubei	83.74
12	Central China	Liaoning	83.26
13	**Shanghai and YRD**	**Anhui**	**82.58**
14	West China	Shaanxi	82.57
15	West China	Guizhou	82.04
16	Central China	Jiangxi	82.27
17	West China	Sichuan	81.64
18	Beijing and Northern China	Hebei	81.61
19	Beijing and Northern China	Jilin	80.41
20	Central China	Inner Mongolia	80.38
21	Central China	Henan	79.69
22	West China	Gansu	79.6
23	Greater PRD	Guangxi	79.18
24	West China	Xinjiang	78.96
25	West China	Ningxia	78.8

(continued)

(continued)

	Region/municipality		Competitiveness ranking (100 = most competitive)
26	Central China	Shanxi	78.3
27	Greater PRD	Hainan	78.3
28	Beijing and Northern China	Heilongjiang	78.23
29	West China	Yunnan	76.49
30	West China	Qinghai	75.88
31	West China	Xizang	73.51

Source Administration of quality supervision, inspection and quarantine, June 2011

Demographics in the YRD

		Anhui (%)	Jiangsu (%)	Zhejiang (%)	Shanghai (%)
Type	Urban	43.0	N/A	61.6	N/A
	Rural	57.0	N/A	38.4	N/A
Gender composition	Male	50.8	50.4	51.4	51.5
	Female	49.2	49.6	48.6	48.5
Age composition	0–14 years	18.0	13.0	13.2	8.6
	15–64 years	71.8	76.1	72.9	81.3
	65 and over	10.2	10.9	13.9	10.1

Sources 2010 Census—communiqué on major data, provincial bureaus of statistics, May 2011

1.6 Infrastructure in the YRD

An important trend in the Yangtze River Delta is that of investment in regional infrastructure, as local governments attempt to better integrate the surrounding economies. Seven state-level comprehensive transportation hubs are being developed in Shanghai, Nanjing, Hangzhou, Ningbo, Wenzhou, Xuzhou and Lianyungang. Projects in the works include improvements both in hardware (transportation networks like waterways, bridges, railways, roads and air) and software (logistics systems and services).

1.6.1 Ports and Waterways

Shipping is the primary source of transportation for non-time sensitive commodities in the Yangtze River Delta. More than 6,300 km long, the Yangtze River is one of the four longest rivers in the world and one of the world's most important cargo-carrying rivers. As well, the river plays an important role in the YRD's manufacturing base, supplying raw materials and components like iron ore, crude oil and coal to factories along the river.

Cargo traffic on the trunk stream of the Yangtze River has grown rapidly from 990 million tons in 2006 to 1.5 billion tons in 2010. There are 220 ports of different sizes along the navigable stretch of the Yangtze River. In recent years, ports have begun to specialize in the transport of particular goods, like metal ore in Nantong and timber in Zhangjiagang.

Local governments have continually pushed for port development and specialization. Between 2006 and 2010, the central government invested RMB13.2 billion to improve the country's waterways, which went to projects like the "digitization of the waterways" and dredging projects in the central provinces.

All of China's busiest river ports are located in the Yangtze River Delta (with the exception of Guangdong's Foshan). Jiangsu's Suzhou is by far the busiest (with cargo throughput double that of the second busiest, Nantong).

1.6.2 Bridges

While the YRD's waterways act as transport routes, they also create the need for bridges to connect separated areas. Notable recent bridge additions include the Sutong Yangtze Bridge between Suzhou and Nantong (operational as of 2008) and the Fourth Nanjing Yangtze Bridge (to be operational in 2012). There will be more than 100 bridges across the Yangtze by 2020, according to Fan Maorun, the chief engineer for the Ministry of Communications.

In addition to cross-river bridges, there are also several large new cross-sea bridges under construction or recently constructed. These include the 32.5 km East China Sea Bridge to the Yangshan Deep Water Port and the 33 km Hangzhou Bay bridge, which reduces driving time between Ningbo and Shanghai to 2 h.

1.6.3 Railroad

Two new high-speed commuter rail lines opened in the YRD in 2010, including the Nanjing–Zhenjiang–Wuxi–Suzhou-Shanghai line and the Shanghai–Jiaxing-Hangzhou line. These lines are part of a larger RMB50 billion investment in over 800 km of new high-speed commuter rail, to be completed by 2020. Such lines are changing the way business is done in the YRD, allowing Shanghai-based managers to keep tabs on operations in nearby second or third tier cities. Travel time between Shanghai and Nanjing is now less than an hour and a half, while travel time between Shanghai and Hangzhou has been reduced to less than an hour.

Another notable rail route is the "New Silk Road," or the New Eurasian Land Bridge, which begins in the port of Liangyungang in northern Jiangsu. Purportedly the shortest route between the Pacific and Atlantic Oceans, this route runs for 10,900 km to Rotterdam through central Asia and utilizes local railway. The route is some 8,000 km shorter than using the Suez Canal sea route and 11,000 km shorter than going across the Pacific through the Panama Canal and across the Atlantic. This route is significant option for transporting containers and bulk cargo from the YRD to Europe.

By 2020, China plans to build a 120,000 km network linking provincial capitals and the nation's larger cities, with trains running at speeds of 200 km an hour or more.

1.6.4 Highways

Highway transportation, with its speed and flexibility, is the main mode of transportation within the YRD. In Jiangsu province, for example, highways account for over 90% of total passenger traffic and about 60–70% of total freight traffic.

A network of highways linking all cities in the YRD is being constructed to shorten traveling time between cities to 3 h or less. These new links have, and will continue to have, a positive effect on longer-haul routes in particular.

1.6.5 Air Freight

Most international airlines and companies specializing in express delivery ser vice offer cargo ser vices to or from China. The number of major international hubs is now increasing and some cheaper air carriers and budget airlines have emerged (i.e. Asia Air). As well, various airports have been undergoing expansions, such as the extension of Hangzhou's airport and the new terminal at Shanghai's Pudong International Airport.

Special Focus: Yangshan Port, Shanghai

Following in the footsteps of the old Shanghai Port built on the Huangpu River in 1843, and the subsequent development of new container terminals in Waigoqiao in the 1990s, the Yangshan project kicked off in 2002. Phase 1, 2 and 3 were completed in 2005, 2006 and 2008 respectively, and the final phase is planned to be fully completed by 2020.

With a natural water depth of 10–15 m, the RMB100 billion project is expected to have an annual handling capacity of 30 million TEUs on completion in 2020. The port is located 32 km from Shanghai and consists of three parts: the container terminals, the Donghai Bridge, and the Luchaogang logistics park. The port and the 32 km-long Donghai Bridge took a mere 3 years to construct at a cost of RMB10 billion so far. The main nautical channel is more than 16 m deep, currently handles 15 million TEUs per annum and is expanding rapidly.

The Shanghai Shengdong International Container Terminal (SSICT) company has pledged to maintain a policy of "5-2-25:" time for handling a barge is no more than 5 h, time for handling a main service vessel no more than 2 h and container delivery to/from the stacking yard is no more than 25 min. The port also boasts a transshipment of 43% (including 11% international), which is also set to rise.

Further construction is required and a number of big projects are in the pipeline—most notably, the new train station at Luchaogang logistics park (the first of its kind in China), which can transport goods to and from the port. Roughly the size of Singapore, the logistics park will house five zones including an industrial and high-tech zone and a 'new city' which will eventually accommodate a population of 500 thousand to 800 thousand by 2020. The bonded logistics area uniquely combines the "inside territory and outside customs" advantage of foreign trade zones with the geographic location advantage of a port. Furthermore, a 10-year project is underway to dredge the Yangtze from Shanghai to Taicang and possibly as far as Nanjing.

In fact, in 2010 Shanghai became the world's busiest port by cargo tonnage throughput, overtaking Singapore. The port is also currently the world's second-largest by container throughput. Yangshan port is expected to contain 50 berths with an annual handling capacity of more than 25 million TEUs by 2020—signs of even bigger things to come.

Chapter 2
Provinces and Cities of the YRD

SHANGHAI
上海

The Pudong business district, Shanghai's "growth engine" east of the historical center of the city, accounts for more than 20 percent GDP.

Dezan Shira & Associates et al. (eds.), *The Yangtze River Delta*, China Briefing,
DOI: 10.1007/978-3-642-27624-8_2, © Asia Briefing Ltd. 2012

Population (million)

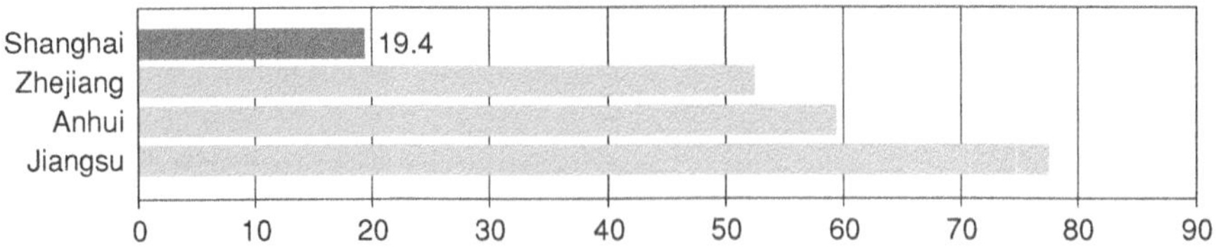

GDP by Industry Level

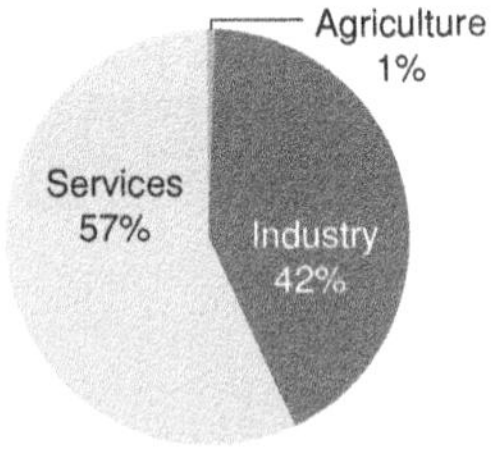

Pillar Industries

- Electronics
- Automotive
- Petrochemical and chemical processing
- Biomedicine

An international metropolis that has witnessed breathtaking economic development, Shanghai shows no signs of slowing down. The city is administratively equal to a province and is divided into 19 county-level divisions. To the north and south are Jiangsu and Zhejiang provinces, while the East China Sea lies to the east, Hangzhou Bay to the south and the Yangtze River to the north.

Since reform and opening, China's State Council and the Shanghai city government have begun to develop the city into an international financial and shipping center, similar in certain ways to Hong Kong. As a result, Shanghai's GDP has been growing extremely fast. In 2009, amidst the financial crisis, Shanghai's GDP rose 8.2% despite official efforts to slow the growth rate to ensure stability and sustainability.

Partially to reduce population density, during the 12th Five-Year Plan (2011–2015) Shanghai will focus on developing seven new satellite cities and developing links with neighboring cities in the Yangtze River Delta. The city is continuing to build up several key industrial sectors (microelectronics, automotive, chemicals, steel, shipbuilding and equipment manufacturing) and aims to draw more foreign investment into six service sectors (modern logistics and transportation, financial services, exhibition and travel services, information services, professional services auxiliary to manufacturing, and entertainment).

2.1 Economy and Investment

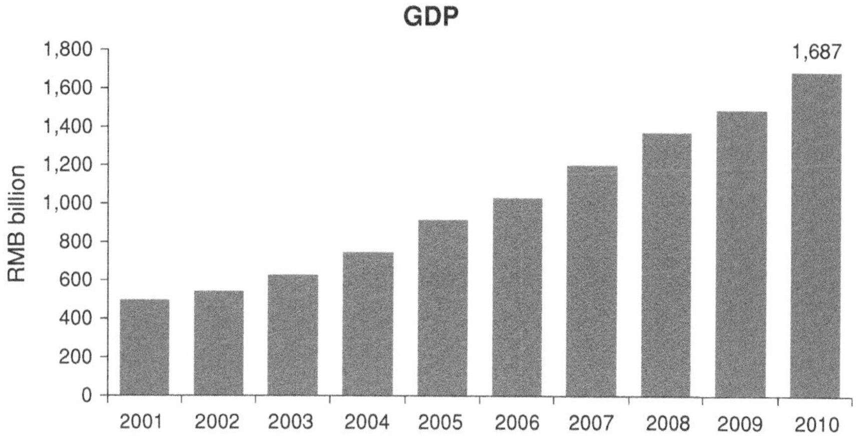

Shanghai is China's largest commercial and trade city. With only 0.1% of the land area of the country, it supplies over 12% of municipal revenue and handles more than a quarter of total trade passing through China's ports. In 2010, Shanghai's GDP reached RMB 1.687 trillion and per capita GDP was RMB 73,294.

Total revenue for Shanghai's retail industry reached RMB 603.7 billion in 2010, with year-on-year growth of 17.5%. Shanghai's mature retail environment and comprehensive municipal infrastructure make it an ideal place to launch a retail enterprise or introduce a brand to China.

Shanghai Stock Exchange

The Shanghai Stock Exchange was founded in 1990 and is the largest stock market on the mainland. In terms of market capitalization, it ranks fifth in the world. There are three main categories of securities listed on the Shanghai Stock Exchange: stocks, bonds and funds. Bonds traded on the exchange include treasury bonds, corporate bonds and convertible corporate bonds. The Shanghai Stock Exchange issues two types of stocks: A shares (priced in RMB) and B shares (priced in USD). Foreign investors can trade B shares without limitations and can trade A shares, with additional limitations, under the Qualified Foreign Institutional Investor system. The exchange plans to eventually merge the two types of shares.

Shanghai also plays host to the Shanghai Futures Exchange. The Shanghai Futures Exchange began operations in May 1999 and was an amalgamation of three exchanges: the Shanghai Metal Exchange, the Shanghai Commodity Exchange and the Shanghai Cereals and Oils Exchange. Contracts are traded for copper, aluminum, zinc, gold, natural rubber and fuel oil.

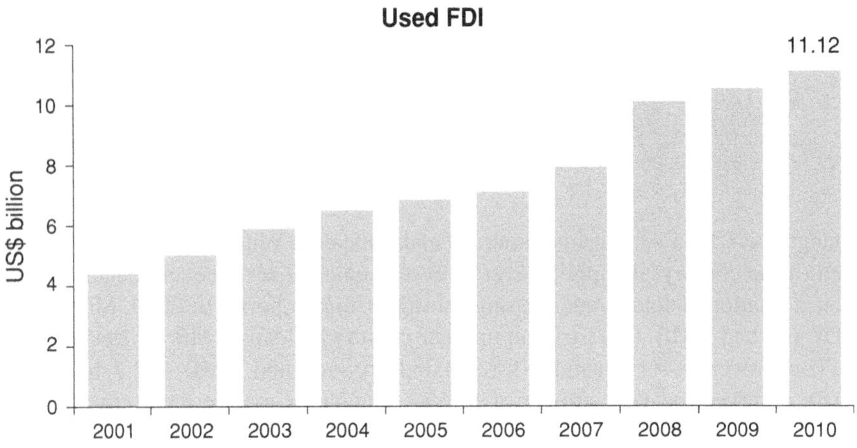

2.2 Infrastructure

2.2.1 Railways

Two major railway lines intersect in the city: the Jinghu railway (connecting Shanghai with Beijing) and the Hu Hang railway (running to Hangzhou).

Shanghai is known for its massive metro system, which transports an average 4.7 million people every day. As of 2011, there are eleven metro lines (excluding the Shanghai Maglev Train) and over 434 km of track in operation, making it the longest network in the world. The local government aspires to have 20 routes by 2020.

The world's first commercial Maglev railway was opened in Shanghai in 2003. It connects Pudong International Airport with the Longyang Road metro station in less than 8 min and reaches a maximum speed of 433 km/h.

2.2.2 Air

Shanghai's airports by passenger throughput (2010)

National rank	Airport	Passenger throughput (# people)	Change y-on-y (%)
3	Pudong	40,578,621	27.1
4	Hongqiao	31,298,812	24.8

Source National Airport Throughput Rankings Civil Aviation Administration of China, March 2011

2.2.3 Ports and Waterways

"Shanghai Port" is actually an amalgamation of three sites: Wusong Port, Waigaoqiao Port and Yangshan Deepwater Port. Yangshan Deepwater Port handles approximately 35% of Shanghai Port's total container throughput (2010).

Despite the addition of Yangshan Port, the throughput of Waigaoqiao Port also continues to rise and it remains a large hub for inter-Asia shipping routes. The older Wusong Port, located on the north end of the Bund, primarily handles domestic container service. The area around the port has most recently been slated for redevelopment to serve cruise liners and possibly yachts.

Shanghai port by throughput (2010)

Goods		Containers	
National rank	Throughput (100 million tons)	National rank	Throughput (million TEU)
2	5.63	1	2,906.93

Source Transportation via public waterways development statistical report, Ministry of Transport, April 2011

2.2.4 Resources

Shanghai City Government
www.shanghai.gov.cn

Shanghai Municipal Commission of Commerce
http://www.scofcom.gov.cn/sfic/en/index.jsp

Shanghai Foreign Investment Service Center
www.sfisc.com

Historical Context

Shanghai literally means "on the sea." The metropolis we see today began as a simple administrative district hundreds of years ago and eventually evolved into an important trading port. During the Ming dynasty in the sixteenth century, the city became the national center for textiles and handicrafts.

Over the course of the next 100 years, Shanghai would become entangled in a delicate tug of war between China's emperors and foreign traders. The First Opium War (1839–1842) ended in defeat for the Chinese and opened Shanghai to foreigners as a treaty port. This, however, triggered the city's first economic boom. Global businesses were being formed in the rapidly expanding trade of cotton and opium. Foreign merchants were eventually followed by diplomats, bureaucrats, assorted professionals and missionaries, and the city soon took on the character of a colony, albeit a slightly unusual one.

By the 1870s, Shanghai had over taken Canton (today known as Guangzhou) as a commercial hub, and by the end of the century it was also a major manufacturing center, reputedly accounting for half of China's modern factory output. Shanghai became a place for Chinese firsts—the first telephones (1881), electricity (1882), running water (1884), cars (1901) and streetcars (1908)—and is in many ways still a trendsetter.

Shanghai weathered the storms of the First and Second World Wars but was deeply influenced by China's tumultuous transition away from dynastic rule. As a colonial enclave and capitalist hub, Shanghai had much to lose from the communist revolution. The manufacturing and commercial base withered away—over 450 factories from Shanghai and nearby cities had been moved west during World War II to protect themselves from the Japanese.

Initially, when the central government began the "reform and opening- up" period in the early 1980s, it ignored Shanghai, preferring to establish Special Economic Zones in southern Chinese cities like Shenzhen.

Deng Xiaoping, Mao's more moderate successor, decided Shanghai's revival was necessary. The city was declared "the new dragon's head" and re-opened for business. Thousands of construction cranes arrived and at one point in the mid-1990s, more than half of all the cranes in the world could be found in Shanghai.

Shanghai by numbers

Item	Unit	2002	2003	2004	2005	2006	2007	2008	2009	2010
Population	m people	16.25	17	17.4	17.78	18.15	18.58	18.8	19.21	23.02
GDP	RMBbn	540.9	625.8	745	914.4	1,029.7	1,200.12	1,369.81	1,490.1	1,687.24
Proportion: primary industry	%	1.4	1.2	1	1	0.9	N/A	0.81	0.8	0.7
: secondary industry	%	45.7	47.9	48.2	48.6	48.5	N/A	45.5	39.9	42.3
: tertiary industry	%	52.9	50.9	50.8	50.4	50.6	21.9	53.6	59.3	57
GDP growth year on year	%	10.9	11.8	13.6	11.1	12	13.3	11.4	8.2	9.9
Per capita GDP (all residents)	RMB	40,646	46,718	55,306	59,600	59,710	60,158	73,126	77,569	73,294
Fixed asset investment	RMBbn	215.84	245.2	308.5	354.3	392.51	445.86	482.31	527.33	531.77
Growth year on year	%	8.2	12.1	25.8	14.8	10.8	13.6	9.3	9.2	0.8
Industrial production value	RMBbn	231.3	286.59	349.3	415.5	464.16	529.6	578.5	540.9	645.7
Growth year on year	%	12.7	17.6	16.1	12.5	13	12.3	9.2	−6.5	17.5
Per capita disposable income of urban residents	RMB	13,250	14,687	16,683	18,645	20,668	23,623	26,690	28,838	31,838
Growth year on year	%	11.5	12.2	12.2	11.8	10.8	14.3	12	8.1	10.4
Retail sales	RMBbn	203.5	222	245	297.3	336	384.8	453.7	517.29	603.69
Growth year on year	%	9.3	9.1	10.5	11.9	13	14.5	14.5	14	17.5
Exports	US$bn	81.8	112.13	161.27	212.43	266.57	328.48	169.2	141.91	180.79
Growth year on year	%	20.3	37.1	43.8	31.7	6.7	23.2	−48	−16.2	27.4
Imports	US$bn	60.7	88.9	121.31	138.25	162.89	192.43	152.6	135.82	188.1
Growth year on year	%	15.7	46.5	36.5	14	17.8	18.1	−21	−11.1	38.5
Contracted FDI	US$bn	10.6	11.1	11.7	13.8	14.574	14.87	17.1	13.3	15.31
Growth year on year	%	0.434	0.235	0.126	0.183	0.054	0.02	15.1	−22.3	15.1
Used FDI(Total)	US$bn	5.03	5.9	6.5	6.85	7.11	7.92	10.1	10.54	11.12
Growth year on year	%	14.5	30.1	11.8	4.7	3.8	11.4	27.4	4.5	5.5
New FIEs	No	3,012	4,321	4,334	4,091	4,061	4,206	3,748	3,090	3,906
Growth year on year	%	22.5	43.5	0.8	−5.6	−0.7	3.6	−10.9	−17.6	26.4

Sources National Bureau of Statistics China Statistical Yearbooks, city government publications, media sources deemed reliable. *N/A* is data not announced in the city government's annual economic and social report and growth data is calculated based on in house data for the previous year. May be available from other sources

JIANGSU PROVINCE
江苏省

Jiangsu's used FDI between 2005 and 2010 was double that during the previous five year period, totaling US$118.2 billion.

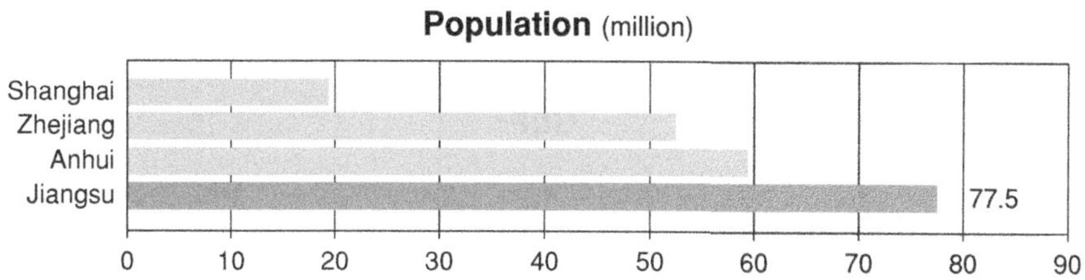

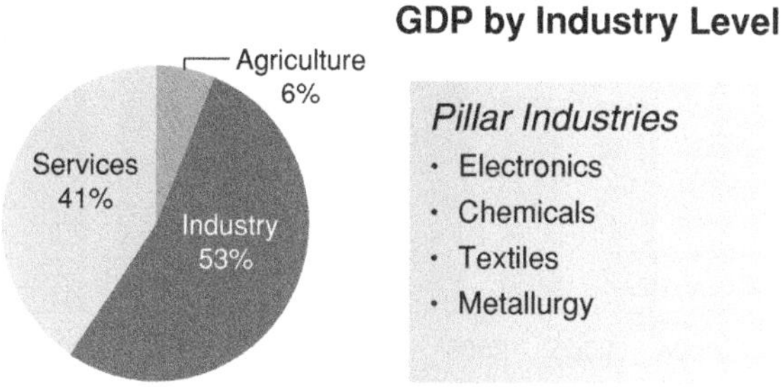

Jiangsu is among the wealthiest provinces in China and has the largest GDP in the Yangtze River Delta. The province also ranks fifth in the National Competitiveness Index,[1] right behind China's major economic players Shanghai, Beijing, Tianjin and Guangdong. The province is home to a well-developed transportation network and in recent years, the development of high-tech, telecommunications and green industries has placed the province in the limelight.

The provincial capital, Nanjing, is known for its prominent role in the nation's history—serving as China's historical capital and falling victim to the brutal Najing Massacre—and as a rising second tier city. The cities of Suzhou, Wuxi and Kunshan in particular, are attracting the attention of foreign investors. Other cities are rising to prominence based on unique merits, such as the city of Huai'an—which ranks first in the nation in terms of education and fifth in terms of healthcare, according to the Economist Intelligence Unit's China—Business City Rankings (November 2010).

The province has seen inconsistent development between its northern and southern regions. The southern part of Jiangsu—including Suzhou, Wuxi, Nanjing and the surrounding area—is booming, while parts of the province north of the Yangtze River remain relatively less developed.

Jiangsu's GDP grew 12.6% in 2010 to RMB 4.09 trillion. Jiangsu also has one of the highest GDPs per capita in the country at RMB 52,360 in 2010. Jiangsu has also become an increasingly important manufacturing base for the IT, petrochemical and

[1] Determined by the Administration of Quality Supervision, Inspection and Quarantine based on present business advantages and future business opportunities, 2010.

pharmaceutical industries. The province is currently the world's leading manufacturer and exporter of solar power equipment, chemicals, electronic equipment, textiles, and certain other types of machinery.

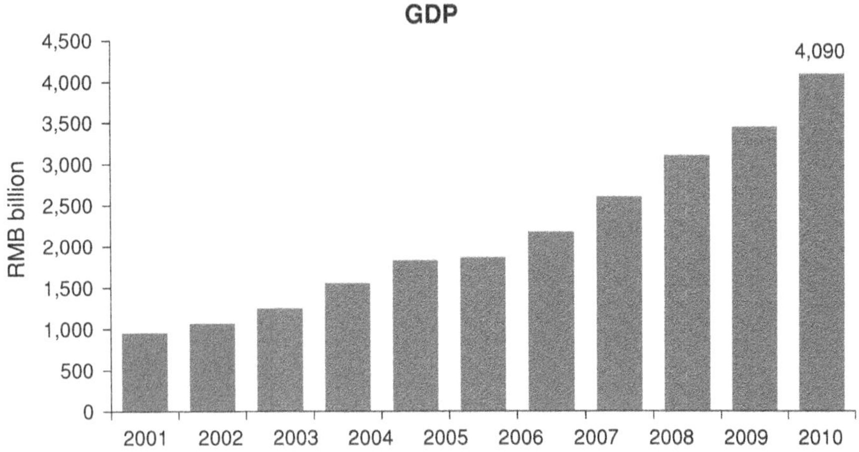

Jiangsu's inroads into the green sector are unparalleled and the province is currently home to the largest number of environmental protection-related firms in mainland China. This is largely due to strong local government support, particularly for windpower development. The province plans to establish 7,000 MW of intertidal and offshore wind farms by 2020. The primary city in this development is Nantong, which has a wind power capacity of 992 MW (2010) and a targeted wind power and installed capacity of 3,000 MW by 2015.

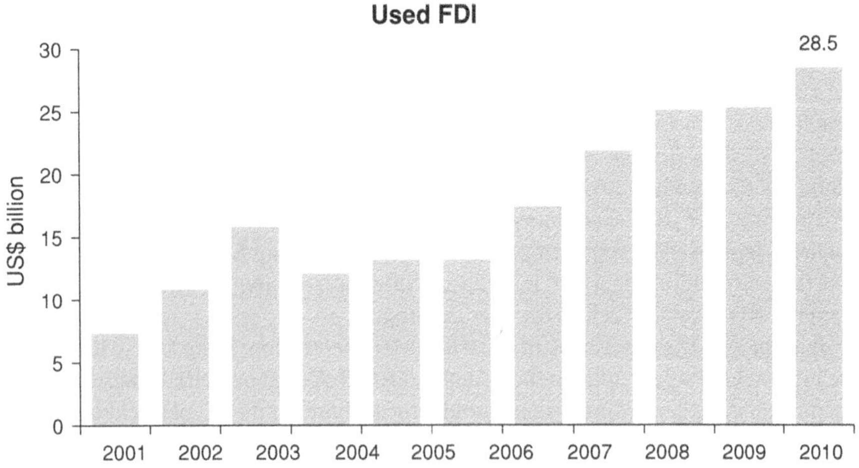

Jiangsu is a popular destination for FDI, utilized FDI increased 12.5% year on year between 2009 and 2010. In particular, Suzhou, Jiangsu province's "Venice of the East," is generating a great deal of excitement among many foreign investors for its popular industrial park.

2.3 Infrastructure

2.3.1 Air

Jiangsu's airports by passenger throughput (2010)

City	Airport	Passenger throughput (# people)	Change y-on-y (%)
Nanjing	Lukou	12,530,515	15.6
Wuxi	Shuofang	2,535,277	14.3
Xuzhou	Guanyin	658,395	28.7
Changzhou	Benniu	658,033	23
Lianyungang	Baitabu	423,031	45.3
Nantong	Hingtung	271,440	23.2
Yancheng	Nanyang	191,336	18.3
Hua'an	Lianshui	39,174	N/A

Source National Airport Throughput Rankings Civil Aviation Administration of China, March 2011

2.3.2 Ports and Waterways

Zhejiang ports and throughput (2010)

Port	Goods		Containers	
	National rank	Throughput (100 million tons)	National rank	Throughput (million TEU)
Sea ports				
Lianyungang	14	1.27		
River ports				
Suzhou	1	3.29	1	364.41
Nantong	2	1.51		
Nanjing	3	1.47	3	145.32
Wuxi	5	1.25	4	101.07
Jiangyin				
Zhenjiang	6	1.06		

Source Transportation via public waterways development statistical report, Ministry of Transport, April 2011

2.3.3 Major Cities

Major cities in Jiangsu (by GDP) include:

- Suzhou
- Wuxi
- Nanjing (Provincial capital)
- Nantong

2.3.4 Resources

Jiangsu Provincial Government
www.js.gov.cn

Historical Context

Jiangsu province was formed in the seventeenth century and before its formation, present day northern Jiangsu and southern Jiangsu had very little to do with one another. Today, southern Jiangsu is generally dominant because it is wealthier and more affluent than the north. Economically the northern and southern portion parts of the province are distinct but there are also unique cultural differences as well. Southern Jiangsu is firmly a part of southern Chinese culture while northern Jiangsu has cultural attributes of both northern and southern China.

Southern Jiangsu emerged as a center of trade during the Song Dynasty (960–1279). At that time, China saw the development of a wealthy mercantile class and emergent market which brought opportunities to the region. Within the same time frame, the local textiles industry began to flourish and some have identified this as the beginnings of industrialization and capitalization in the heart of present day China, which was ultimately abandoned before being adopted in the West.

Culture flourished in the region during the period of the Six Dynasties (220–589) when an influx of immigrants from the north arrived. Jiangsu is considered a gateway to central China and this prime location launched the province as a key cultural hub and the main scene of European commercial activity after the Treaty of Nanjing in 1842. These historical events have contributed to southern Jiangsu's present day reputation of wealth and affluence.

Jiangsu has had its fair share of conflict as well. Like many other provinces in the Yangtze River Delta region, it was seriously affected by the Taiping Rebellion (1850–1864). Nanjing even became the Taiping capital in 1853 and remained so for more than a decade.

Jiangsu province by numbers

	Unit	2002	2003	2004	2005	2005	2006	2007	2008	2009	2010
Population	m people	73.81	74.06	74.33	74.75	49	49.8	50.6	76.8	77.3	78.1
GDP	RMBbn	1,063.63	1,245.18	1,551.24	1,827.21	1,859.90	2,174.20	2,601.80	3,098.20	3,445.70	4090.3
Proportion: primary industry	%	10.6	8.9	N/A	7.6	7.9	7.1	7	6.8	6.6	6.2
: secondary industry	%	52.1	54.5	N/A	56.6	56.6	56.5	55.6	54.8	56.9	53.2
: tertiary industry	%	37.3	36.6	N/A	35.8	35.6	36.4	37.4	38.4	39.6	40.6
GDP growth year on year	%	11.6	13.5	14.9	14.5	24	16.9	19.7	19.1	11.2	12.6
Per capita GDP (all residents)	RMB	14,397	16,796	20,000	24,515	24,953	28,943	34,294	40,499	44,744	52,360
Fixed asset investment	RMBbn	384.92	533.58	682.76	873.97	874	1,007.10	1,226.80	1,506.00	1,895.00	2318.7
Growth year on year	%	16.5	38.6	28	28	28	15.2	21.8	22.8	25.8	22.4
Industrial production value	RMBbn	482.01	522.49	644.75	932.667	944	1,109.80	1,310.50	1,527.10	1,646.50	2122.4
Growth year on year	%	14	8.4	23.4	16.7	25.6	17.6	18.1	16.5	7.8	16
Per capita disposable income of urban residents	RMB	8,178	7,940	10,482	12,319	12,319	14,084	16,378	18,680	20,552	22944
Growth year on year	%	10.9	−2.9	13.2	17.5	11	10.2	12.9	12.1	8.8	9.2
Retail sales	RMBbn	321.58	356.7	415.97	569.99	573.5	670.6	798.6	990.5	1,148.40	1348.2
Growth year on year	%	12.1	10.9	16.6	16	17.2	16.9	19.1	24	15.9	18.7
Exports	US$bn	38.48	59.14	87.56	122.982	123	160.4	203.7	238	199.2	270.6
Growth year on year	%	33	53.7	48.1	40.5	40.6	30.4	27	16.8	−16.3	35.8
Imports	*US$bn*	31.82	54.53	83.25	104.959	105	123.6	145.9	154.2	139.6	195.2
Growth year on year	%	41.6	71.3	52.7	26.1	25.9	17.7	18.1	5.7	−9.5	39.9
Contracted FDI	US$bn	19.67	30.81	36.1	45.72	46.4	46.5	52.7	50.7	51	56.83
Growth year on year	%	132.8	56.6	17.1	18.5	28.5	0.2	13.3	−3.8	0.6	11.5
Used FDI	US$bn	10.83	15.8	12.1	13.18	13.18	17.43	21.89	25.12	25.32	28.5
Growth year on year	%	76.3	52.4	14.5	29.2	8.6	32.2	25.6	14.7	0.8	12.5
New FIEs	No	5,801	7,301	N/A	N/A	N/A	6,541	5,986	4,236	4,219	4661
Growth year on year	%	70	25.9	N/A	N/A	N/A	N/A	−8.5	−29.2	−0.4	10.5

Sources National Bureau of Statistics China Statistical Yearbooks, city government publications, media sources deemed reliable. *N/A* is data not announced in the city government's annual economic and social report and growth data is calculated based on in house data for the previous year. May be available from other sources

Changzhou 常州

Innovative Municipal Government

Changzhou was selected as the city with the most innovative municipal government in the 2009 National City Competitiveness Rankings.

A Qing dynasty poet declared "there are none such under heaven as Changzhou." Today, the city is emerging as a destination for foreign investment. As land and labor prices rise in cities like Shanghai and Suzhou, more and more investors are looking at Changzhou, only 2 h from Shanghai via train, as an alternative location to set up business.

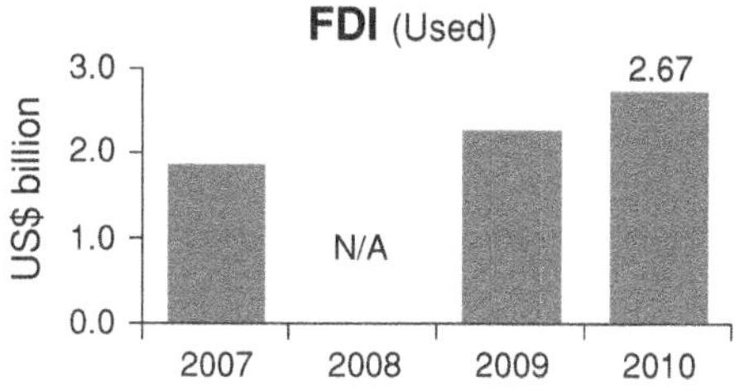

Used FDI was US$2.67 billion in 2010, a 18.1 percent growth year-on-year.

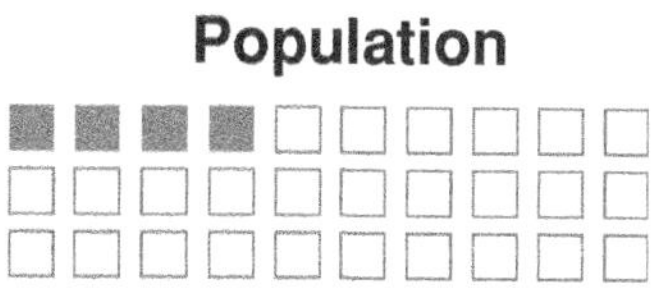

3.6 million

2.4 Infrastructure

2.4.1 Railways

The Changzhou Railway Station is one of the key stops on the busy Shanghai–Nanjing route. In July 2011, the city became connected to the Beijing–Shanghai high-speed railway, granting quick service to major cities (40 min to Shanghai, four and a half hours to Beijing).

2.4.2 Ports and Waterways

Although not as large as Shanghai or Nanjing, Changzhou has a Category A cargo transport port. Five 10,000-ton deep-water berths have opened in recent years and another four 10,000-ton deep-water berths will open in 2011–2012. A total port cargo throughput of 31.64 million tons was achieved in 2010, an increase of 15.9%, and the number of containers handled reached 11,301, an increase of 60.7%.

2.5 Economy and Investment

Changzhou's FDI is the third highest in Jiangsu province (behind Suzhou and Wuxi) and the fifth highest in the YRD, according to the National Statistics Bureau (2009).

The city also has the sixth best economy in China according to the Economist Intelligence Unit China-Business Full City Rankings, November 2010 (see source for ranking details).

In total, there are 51 Fortune 500 companies that have set up their offices in Changzhou. Fortune 500 companies in the city include: GE, Bosch, Texas Instruments, Goodyear, Suzuki, Toshiba, Hitachi, Fujitsu, Bridgestone, Hyundai, Auchan, Metro, Carrefour, Walmart, and Tesco. In 2010, seven of the city's 32 foreign-invested projects came from Fortune 500 companies.

Development zones are a huge draw in the city—among the 172 new major investment projects in 2010, 104 were formed in development zones. There are over 28,000 manufacturing enterprises in Changzhou, with the main industries being agricultural machinery manufacturing, electricity transmission and transformation equipment manufacturing, engineering machinery and vehicle manufacturing and new style textile garments.

Changzhou has long been an important manufacturing base for diesel engines, high-speed locomotives, transformers, DVDs, clothing, and engineering machinery. In recent times, Changzhou's government has placed more emphasis on its high-tech, electronic, biomedical and chemical productions. The city has a number of commodities markets, including Lin Jiatang Market, Changjiang Plastic Chemical Market and Wutong Textile City.

In addition, Changzhou is known for its flourishing animation industry. As of 2010, Changzhou has built three large-scale animation production parks within the city. So far, these parks have attracted nearly 60 enterprises and investments of almost RMB 300 million.

Spotlight: sales revenue goals for 2015

	Sales revenue in 2015	Avg. annual increase (%)
All emerging industrial enterprises	RMB 1.39 trillion	28
New energy	RMB 270 billion	30
High-end equipment manufacturing	RMB 540 billion	26
Advanced materials	RMB 350 billion	27
Biotechnology and new medicine	RMB 85 billion	34
Energy-saving env. protection	RMB 75 billion	32
Software and service outsourcing	RMB 40 billion	30

Source Changzhou municipal bureau of commerce, Changzhou investment environment annual 2011

Changzhou's exports to the EU and ASEAN countries increased significantly in 2010, up 60.8 and 51.3% year-on-year, to US $4.6 billion and US $1.42 billion respectively.

2.5.1 Resources

Changzhou Government
http://www.changzhou.gov.cn/

Changzhou National High-Tech District Foreign Investment Promotional Bureau
http://www.invest-in-cnd.cn/newEbiz1/EbizPortalFG/portal/html/index.html

Key Industries

- High tech
- Advanced equipment manufacturing
- Electronics and information technology
- Renewable energy and environmental protection
- Advanced materials
- Biotechnology and pharmaceutical Industries

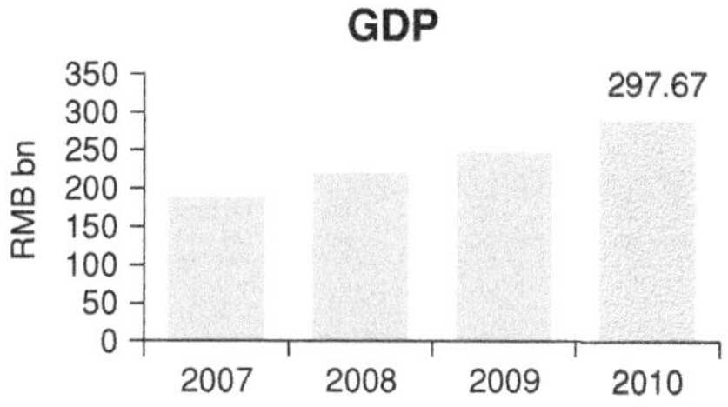

Changzhou's GDP was RMB297.67 billion in 2010, a 18.2 percent growth year-on-year.

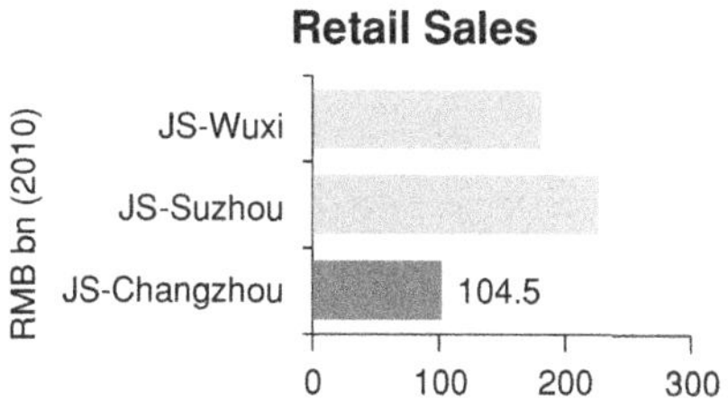

Changzhou's retail sales reached RMB104.5 billion in 2010, lower than many surrounding cities.

Changzhou by numbers

Item	Unit	2002	2003	2004	2005	2006	2007	2008	2009	2010
Population	m people	3.432	3.462	3.489	3.516	3.547	3.57	3.59	3.6	3.6
GDP	RMBbn	76.03	90.02	110	130.22	156	188	220.2	251.87	297.67
Proportion: primary industry	%	6.5	5.2	4.7	4.3	3.8	3.4	3.1	3.6	3.4
: secondary industry	%	56.7	57.7	58.8	61.1	61	59.6	58.9	56.8	56
: tertiary industry	%	36.8	37.1	36.5	34.6	35.2	37	38	39.6	40
GDP growth year on year	%	12.4	18.4	22.2	18.4	19.8	20.5	17.1	14.4	18.2
Per capita GDP (all residents)	RMB	22,260	26,110	31,665	37,174	37,210	52,805	50,283	56,861	65,000
Fixed asset investment	RMBbn	25	44.66	58.86	76.98	95.16	120.39	144.82	170.48	210.36
Growth year on year	%	31.1	78.6	31.8	30.8	23.6	26.5	20.3	17.7	23.4
Industrial production value	RMBbn	165	214.15	275.43	340	422.71	524.33	520	597.87	738.78
Growth year on year	%	16	29.8	28.6	23.4	24.3	24	−0.8	15	23.6
Per capita disposable income of urban residents	RMB	10,759	11,307	12,868	14,589	16,649	19,089	21,592	23,751	26,269
Growth year on year	%	14.4	5.1	13.8	13.4	14.1	14.7	13.1	10	10.6
Retail sales	RMBbn	24.95	28.06	32.41	44.41	51.58	61.1	75.82	90.14	104.47
Growth year on year	%	12.1	12.5	15.5	37	16.1	18.5	24.1	18.9	15.9
Exports	US$bn	2.66	3.53	4.72	6.12	7.89	9.85	13.24	10.87	15.56
Growth year on year	%	22.7	32.7	33.7	29.7	28.9	24.8	34.4	−17.9	43.1
Imports	US$bn	1.26	1.72	2.19	2.21	2.55	3.38	4.39	4.21	6.72
Growth year on year	%	15.5	36.5	27.3	0.9	15.4	32.5	29.9	−4.1	59.6
Contracted FDI	US$bn	2.57	2.05	2.2	2.85	3.3	4.4	3.41	N/A	N/A
Growth year on year	%	122	-20.2	7.3	29.5	15.8	33.3	−22.5	N/A	N/A
Used FDI	US$bn	0.98	0.86	0.58	0.73	1.25	1.83	N/A	2.26	2.67
Growth year on year	%	58.2	−12.2	−32.6	25.9	71.2	46.4	N/A	10.9	18.1
New FIEs	No	363	533	438	N/A	505	401	245	N/A	N/A
Growth year on year	%	N/A	N/A	N/A	N/A	N/A	N/A	N/A	N/A	N/A

Sources National Bureau of Statistics China Statistical Yearbooks, city government publications, media sources deemed reliable. *N/A* is data not announced in the city government's annual economic and social report and may be available from other sources. Growth data is calculated based on in house data for the previous year and may differ from other sources

Nanjing 南京

Historical Southern Capital

Nanjing, which means "southern capital," is the capital of the Jiangsu Province and served as the capital of China at several points in history

Nanjing is a key strategic logistics hub in the Yangtze River Delta. Its position at a key point between two major development belts—the north/south coastal megalopolis and the east/west Yangtze River basin—has enabled it to build extensive transportation infrastructure. Nanjing's Lukou airport is 10th in China in cargo and mail throughput (2010), according to the Civil Aviation Administration.

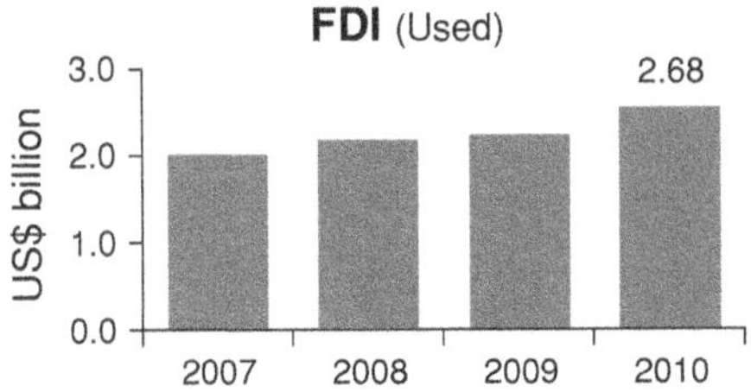

Used FDI reached US$2.68 billion in 2010, with 387 new foreign-invested enterprises.

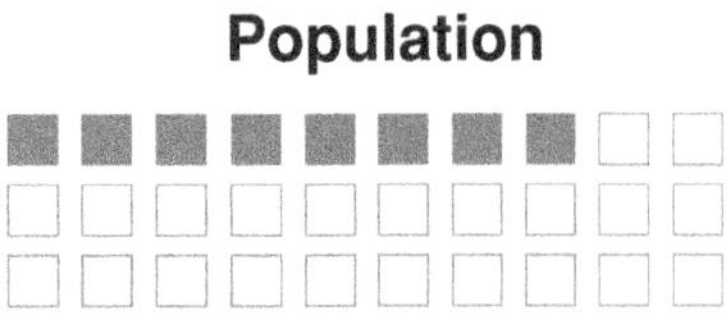

8 million

2.6 Infrastructure

2.6.1 Railways

The city is an important hub for railways linking North, East and Central China. The Shanghai–Nanjing line was upgraded to high-speed service in July 2010 and the journey time between the two cities has been cut to just over 73 min. The Nanjing South Station was opened in June 2011. The station, which is five times larger than the older Nanjing Station, connects the city to the nation's high-speed rail network, including the Beijing–Shanghai high-speed railway, Nanjing–Hangzhou high-speed railway, Shanghai–Wuhan–Chengdu high-speed railway, Nanjing–Anqing high-speed railway and Nanjing–Nantong high-speed railway.

2.6.2 Ports and Waterways

The port of Nanjing is the largest inland port in China, with eighteen 10,000-DWT wharfs, fifty-two 1,000-DWT wharfs and sixteen buoy berths. The port also has 59 km^2 of warehouses, 48 km^2 of storage yards, and an 18 km port railway. The Port of Nanjing is the largest center for trade in petrochemicals, coal and container shipping along the Yangtze River, and altogether had a cargo throughput of 72 million tons and container throughput of 1.44 million TEUs in 2010. These figures are expected to more than double in the next 5 years.

2.7 Economy and Investment

While once a primary hub for culture and politics in the early twentieth century, Nanjing came into the new millennium with a larger focus on economic development. The city is known as an OEM manufacturing base that is able to source products regionally.

Due in large part to its proximity to Shanghai, Nanjing enjoys the attention of many foreign companies looking to set up manufacturing businesses. Investments include those from companies such as Siemens, Shell, Ericsson, Ford, Motorola, Sharp and Samsung. Yet Nanjing is facing fierce competition from neighboring cities, such as Wuxi, Suzhou and Hangzhou.

Nanjing is also emerging as a target for foreign companies looking to sell to the Chinese market. The city ranked 10th in terms of sales of social consumer goods nationally according to the National Statistics Bureau (2009) and disposable income per capita grew 11% to RMB 28,312 in 2010.

Nanjing also has hopes to enhance its reputation as a center of research and technology, and has drawn plans to attract overseas talent and innovation to the city. In 2011, the city initiated the '1000-Talents Program,' which offered foreign experts various positions in local universities and research institutions, as well as generous incentives.

Nanjing's exports are growing, particularly in terms of foreign-funded enterprises, and the high-tech and mechanical/electrical product sectors. Foreign-funded enterprises reached US $8.351 billion annual export value in 2010, up 28.8% year-on-year, and accounting for 33.6% of city's total exports. High-tech exports reached US $6.928 billion, an increase of 37.8% year- on-year, while mechanical and electrical product exports were US $13.576 billion, an increase of 36.3% year-on-year.

2.7.1 Spotlight: Nanjing Finance Town

In mid-2011, Nanjing started construction of its "Finance Town," a development area for international business services and finance companies. It will be located in the central area of Nanjing's developing Hexi district. The development will cover about 80 km^2, and is expected to be a base for many large office buildings and skyscrapers. Total investment in the project was estimated to be around RMB 7 billion.

2.7.2 Resources

Nanjing Government
http://www.nanjing.gov.cn/

Key Industries

- Electronics
- Automotive
- Pharmaceuticals
- Petrochemicals
- Steel
- Power

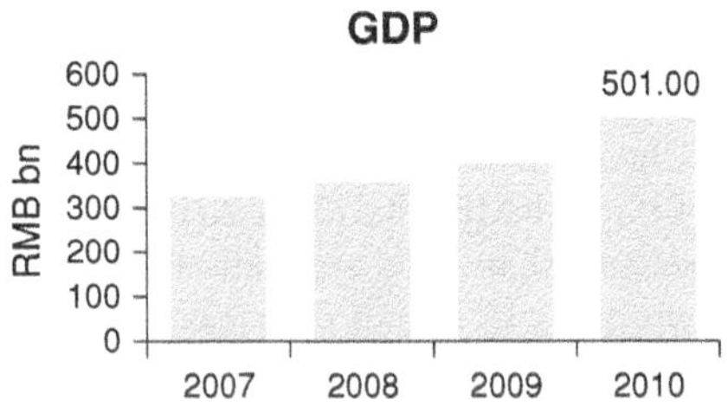

In 2010, the city's GDP reached RMB501 billion, up 13.1 percent from the previous year.

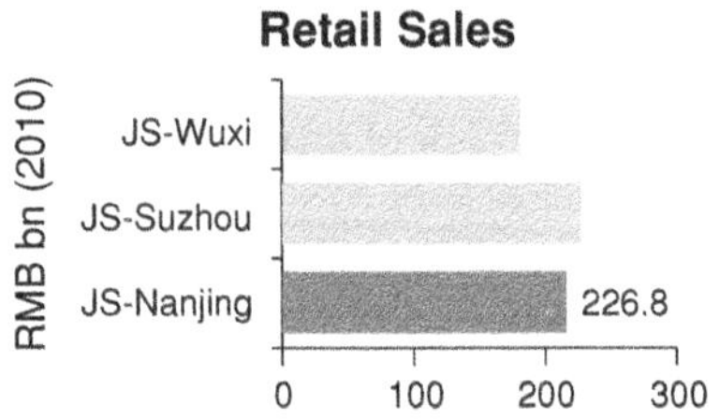

Nanjing's retail sales reached RMB226.8 billion in 2010, high for the region (but below Suzhou).

Nanjing by numbers

Item	Unit	2002	2003	2004	2005	2006	2007	2008	2009	2010
Population	m people	5.63	6.43	6.90	N/A	7.19	7.41	7.59	7.71	8.00
GDP	RMBbn	129.50	157.62	191.00	241.30	277.40	327.50	377.50	423.30	501.00
Proportion: primary industry	%	4.80	4.10	3.70	3.30	3.00	2.60	2.50	3.10	2.80
: secondary industry	%	47.30	51.00	52.60	50.40	49.50	49.00	47.50	45.60	46.50
: tertiary industry	%	47.90	44.90	43.70	46.30	47.50	48.40	50.00	51.30	50.70
GDP growth year on year	%	12.22	21.71	21.18	26.34	14.96	18.06	15.27	12.13	18.36
Per capita GDP (all residents)	RMB	23,002	24,513	27,681	N/A	38,581	44,197	49,736	54,903	62,625
Fixed asset investment	RMBbn	60.30	95.40	120.20	140.27	161.36	186.80	215.42	266.80	330.61
Growth year on year	%	29.71	58.21	26.00	16.70	15.04	15.77	15.32	23.85	23.92
Industrial production value	RMBbn	N/A	N/A	N/A	N/A	469.50	579.16	647.22	676.00	850.00
Growth year on year	%	N/A	N/A	N/A	N/A	16.20	23.36	11.75	4.45	25.74
Per capita disposable income of urban residents	RMB	9,157	10,196	11,602	14,997	17,538	20,317	23,122	25,504	28,312
Growth year on year	%	3.49	11.35	13.79	29.26	16.94	15.85	13.81	10.30	11.01
Retail sales	RMBbn	52.52	60.00	71.14	100.50	116.70	138.05	165.18	196.16	226.78
Growth year on year	%	12.70	14.24	18.57	41.27	16.12	18.29	19.65	18.76	15.61
Exports	US$bn	6.01	7.67	10.46	14.25	17.37	20.65	23.60	18.46	24.89
Growth year on year	%	4.54	27.60	36.38	36.23	21.89	18.88	14.29	−21.78	34.83
Imports	US$bn	4.08	7.05	10.18	12.85	14.17	15.55	17.00	15.29	20.71
Growth year on year	%	6.25	72.79	44.40	26.23	10.27	9.74	9.32	−10.06	35.45
Contracted FDI	US$bn	2.17	4.00	4.50	5.13	3.08	3.79	4.46	4.56	4.78
Growth year on year	%	141.11	84.33	12.50	14.00	−39.96	23.05	17.68	2.24	4.82
Used FDI	US$bn	N/A	2.21	2.60	1.42	1.70	2.06	2.37	2.39	2.68
Growth year on year	%	NA	47.20	17.65	−45.38	19.72	21.18	15.05	0.84	12.13
New FIEs	No	646.00	N/A	803.00	728.00	604.00	N/A	N/A	N/A	387.00
Growth year on year	%	57.56	N/A	N/A	−9.34	-17.03	N/A	N/A	N/A	N/A

Sources National Bureau of Statistics China Statistical Yearbooks, city government publications, media sources deemed reliable. *N/A* is data not announced in the city government's annual economic and social report and may be available from other sources. Growth data is calculated based on in house data for the previous year and may differ from other sources

Suzhou 苏州

FDI Sweetheart

In the immensely popular Suzhou Industrial Park, built in cooperation with Singapore, standard factory rental rates rival those in Shanghai.

Nicknamed "Venice of the East," Suzhou has long had a reputation for beautiful landscapes, but more recently Suzhou has gained a name as an FDI haven. Suzhou's FDI is the fourth highest in China (below Shanghai, Ordos and Tianjin, 2009) according to the National Bureau of Statistics. Much of this FDI has been directed into Suzhou Industrial Park or aimed at the city's high disposable incomes.

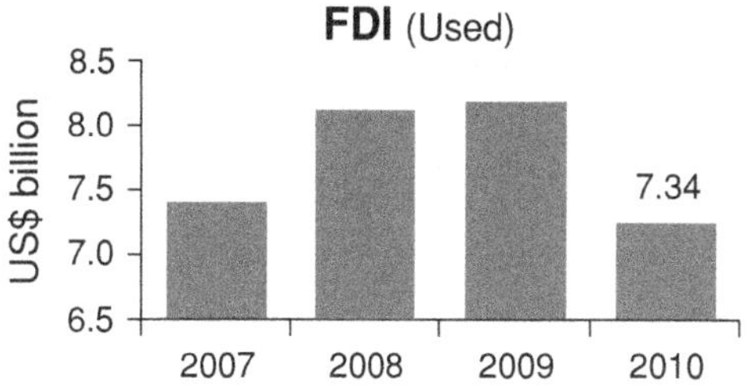

Used FDI was US$7.34 billion in 2010, with 1,537 new foreign-invested enterprises established - the highest in the province.

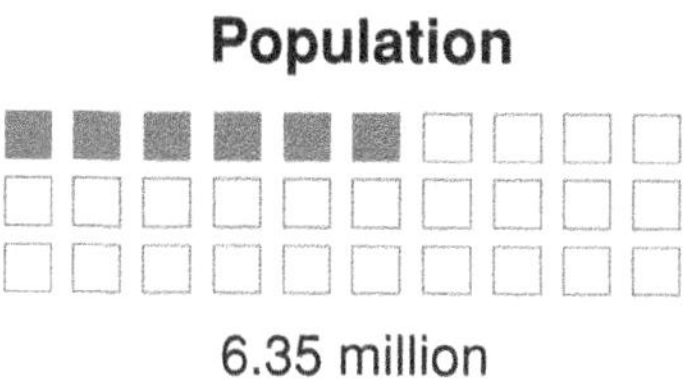

2.8 Infrastructure

Suzhou is set to continue to expand in the next 10 years. The downtown area will be expanded into an area surrounded by highways, while the western boundary will be extended 1 km towards Lake Tai.

2.8.1 Railways

Suzhou is an important city on the Beijing–Shanghai railway line as well as the Jinghu railway, linking Shanghai and Nanjing. There is an hourly railway service to both cities. D-series trains (dongche) connect to Shanghai in 45 min and to Nanjing in 90 min. G-series trains (gaotie), which have been in operation since July 2010, connect to Shanghai station and Shanghai Hongqiao station in 25 min.

2.8.2 Ports and Waterways

China's Grand Canal, which reaches north to Tong County in Beijing as well as south to Jiaxing and Hangzhou in Zhejiang Province, passes by Suzhou and has been an important means of water transportation for centuries.

Suzhou Port, founded in 2002, consists of Zhangjiagang Port (90 km from Suzhou), Changshu Port (62 km from Suzhou) and Taicang Port (72 km from Suzhou). While Suzhou's port is ranked sixth nationally in terms of general cargo and tenth nationally by TEU throughput, the majority of trade for Suzhou is carried out at Shanghai Port (120 km from Suzhou).

Suzhou has the second highest imports and exports of any city in China (lower than Shanghai, but higher than even Shenzhen, Beijing and Guangzhou) according to the National Bureau of Statistics (2009).

2.9 Economy and Investment

Suzhou ranked fifth nationally in the Forbes Magazine "Best Cities for Business in Mainland China" (2010). I n addition to capturing the overflow of many companies who find Shanghai too expensive, many suppliers of Shanghai manufacturers are located in Suzhou's surrounding area. Many foreign executives manage operations based in Suzhou from Shanghai.

As the most economically developed city in Jiangsu Province, Suzhou outperformed some other major cities like Guangzhou in trade performance and realized total imports and exports of US $274.1 billion in 2010. This figure is close to the level of trade volume in the country's other vibrant metropolises such as Shanghai, Beijing and Shenzhen.

The Suzhou Industrial Park (SIP), responsible for 15% of the economic output of the city, holds a business presence for more than 82 Fortune 500 companies (2009). Key advantages offered to investors include:

- Business tax exemption for revenue from offshore service outsourcing
- Refunds (no less than 50%) of retained individual income tax for expatriate high-level managers at headquarters or regional headquarters of service outsourcing companies
- No limit on foreign investment approval; SIP can independently approve the project as long as investment meets the state industry policies
- Excellent and exclusive regional social security system that covers multiple insurance items with one provident fund, modeled after Singapore's Central Provident Fund
- A complete modern logistics system—SIP is one of the first export processing zones approved by the state, giving it independence from customs

2.9.1 Resources

Suzhou Government
www.eng.suzhou.gov.cn/english/index.shtml

China-Singapore Suzhou Industrial Park
www.sipac.gov.cn/english/

Key Industries

2011–2015, SIP will be focusing on:

- Manufacturing (IT and precision machinery)
- Services (finance, headquarter, culture, outsourcing, logistics and convention)
- Nanotech
- Rising Innovation Sectors (optical energy, biomed, converged communications, software/animation and ecological protection)

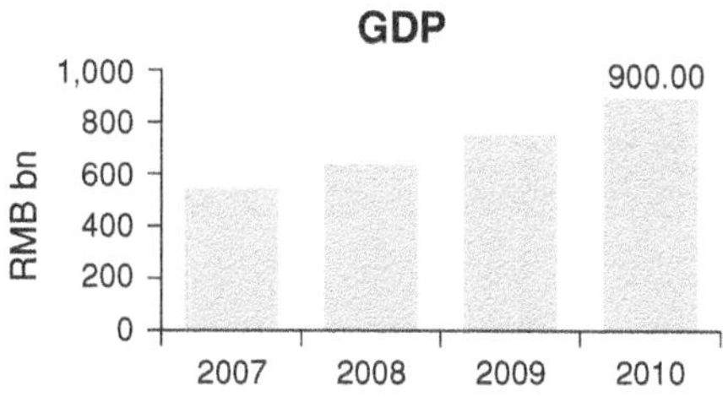

Suzhou's GDP was RMB900 billion in 2010, a 16.3 percent growth year-on-year.

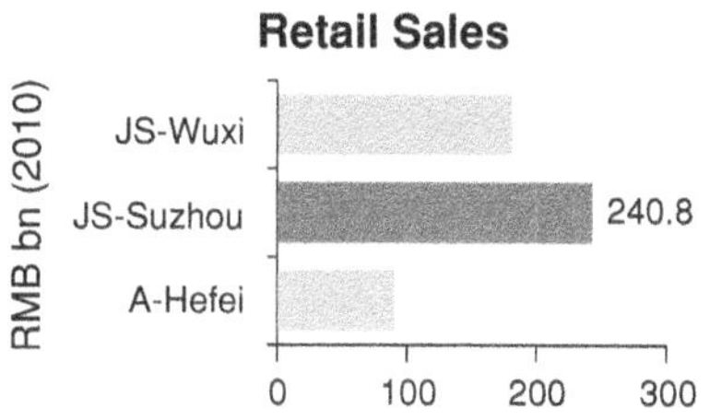

Suzhou's retail sales reached RMB240.8 billion in 2010, highest in the province.

Suzhou by numbers

Item	Unit	2002	2003	2004	2005	2006	2007	2008	2009	2010
Population	m people	5.83	5.9	5.99	6.07	6.16	6.24	6.29	6.33	6.35
GDP	RMBbn	208	280.2	345	402.65	482.03	570	670.1	774	900
Proportion: primary industry	%	4.5	2.8	2.2	6.6	1.9	1.7	1.6	1.8	1.7
: secondary industry	%	58.1	63.1	65.7	69.1	65.4	63.7	62	58.8	57.7
: tertiary industry	%	37.4	34.1	32.1	49.3	32.7	34.6	36.4	39.4	40.6
GDP growth year on year	%	14.5	34.7	23.1	16.7	19.7	18.2	17.6	11	16.3
Per capita GDP (all residents)	RMB	35,678	47,492	57,596	66,335	78,252	91,346	106,534	122,275	141,732
Fixed asset investment	RMBbn	81	140.9	155.5	187	210.7	236	261.12	296.7	361.8
Growth year on year	%	43.4	74	10.4	20.3	12.7	12.0	10.6	13.6	21.9
Industrial production value	RMBbn	508.7	701.08	956.13	1,210	1,531.6	1,904	2,210	2,370.05	2,848
Growth year on year	%	24.8	37.8	36.4	26.6	26.6	24.3	16.1	7.2	20.2
Per capita disposable income of urban residents	RMB	10,617	12,361	14,451	16,276	18,532	21,260	23,867	26,320	29,219
Growth year on year	%	10.2	16.4	16.9	12.6	13.9	14.7	12.3	10.3	11
Retail sales	RMBbn	45.16	52.6	62.51	82.14	105.5	124.55	155.18	202.7	240.8
Growth year on year	%	15.3	16.5	18.8	31.4	28.4	18.1	24.6	30.6	18.8
Exports	US$bn	18.52	32.63	50.77	70	94.69	118	131.7	114.1	153.11
Growth year on year	%	50.5	76.2	55.6	37.9	35.3	24.6	11.6	−13.4	34.19
Imports	US$bn	17.87	33.03	52.43	70	79.58	95	96.8	87.4	112.17
Growth year on year	%	58	84.8	58.7	33.5	13.7	19.4	1.9	−9.7	28.3
Contracted FDI	US$bn	10.1	12.5	14.1	15.34	16	18.52	16.34	13.16	13.528
Growth year on year	%	144.6	23.8	12.8	8.8	4.3	15.8	−11.8	−19.4	2.8
Used FDI	US$bn	4.814	6.805	9.5	6.005	6.17	7.38	8.13	8.2	7.34
Growth year on year	%	59.3	41.4	39.6	−36.8	2.7	19.6	10.2	0.9	−10.5
New FIEs	No	2,019	N/A	N/A	N/A	N/A	1,017	N/A	1426	1537
Growth year on year	%	N/A	N/A	N/A	N/A	N/A	N/A	N/A	−3.37	6.83

Sources National Bureau of Statistics China Statistical Yearbooks, city government publications, media sources deemed reliable. *N/A* is data not announced in the city government's annual economic and social report and may be available from other sources. Growth data is calculated based on in house data for the previous year and may differ from other sources

One of Suzhou's Logistics Departments

Changshu 常熟

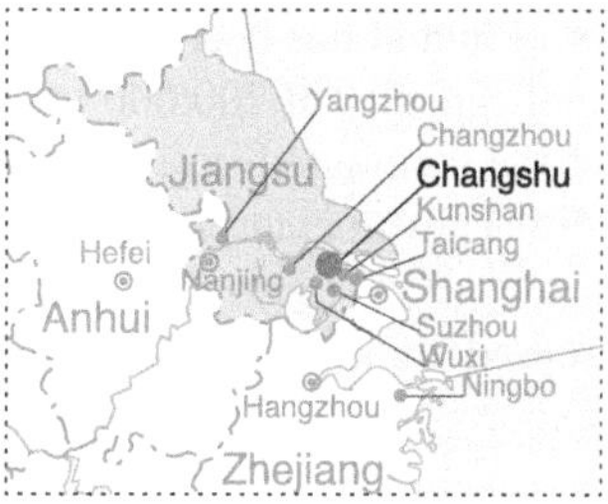

Changshu's has one of the highest levels of imports and exports among all of China's administrative regions, totaling US$11.67 billion (2009).

2.10 Infrastructure

2.10.1 Ports and Waterways

Changshu Port is ranked as one of the ten busiest river ports in China and supports both Shanghai Port and the Suzhou Industrial Park. Changshu Port was opened in 1996 to international vessels and since then has been one of the fastest growing ports in the YRD. Changshu Port has 30 all-purpose berths and 17 of them allow the anchorage of over 10,000-DWT ships. Changshu Port reported a 13% increase in conventional cargoes in 2010 and claims to be the leading hub for steel, pulp, paper and logs in China.

2.10.2 Spotlight: Changshu Economic Development Zone

As a national-level development zone, CEDZ boasts greater autonomy from local and central governments. Industries of focus within this zone include machinery, automobiles, new energy and fine chemicals. Customs clearance services, commodity inspection, warehousing and tax incentives are available in the export processing zone located in the CEDZ. The New and High-Tech Industrial Park, under the zone, is a growing hub for high-tech development in Changshu.

2.11 Economy and Investment

Changshu is located in an economically rich area, and while its GDP pales slightly compared to the GDPs of neighboring Wuxi (RMB 499 billion), Nanjing (RMB 423 billion) or Changzhou (RMB 297 billion), its GDP of RMB 145 billion is growing fast, 18% year-on-year between 2009 and 2010.

The city's major industries include textiles, papermaking, fine chemicals, machinery, steel and forestry. Changshu has a reputation as a textile base and the "Changshu Garments Town of China" is the largest wholesale base of its kind in China.

More than 2,000 foreign enterprises have invested in Changshu, including big names such as Sharp and Dunlop. UMP-Kymmene from Finland has been running a papermill in the city since 1999 and now has an annual capacity of 200,000 tons of coated and 600,000 tons of uncoated fine paper. Of the contracted investment, at least one-third has come from Taiwan—more than 500 Taiwan enterprises have invested more than US $100 million in the city.

Changshu's import and export rate has also increased in recent years with imports going up by 49.3% to US $5.67 billion and exports rising 48.82% to US $11.66 billion in 2010.

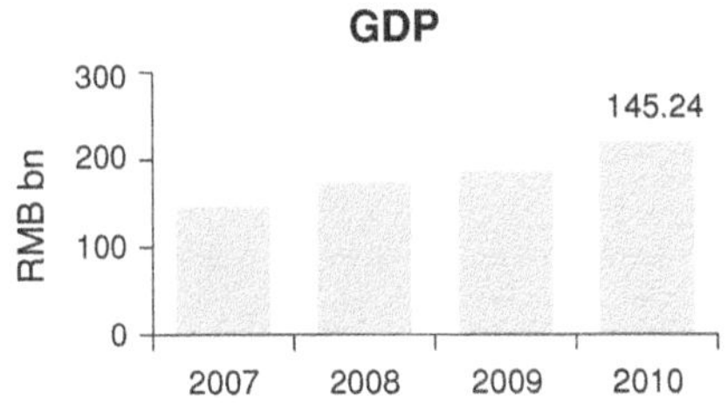

GDP was RMB145.24 billion in 2010, an 18 percent growth rate year-on-year.

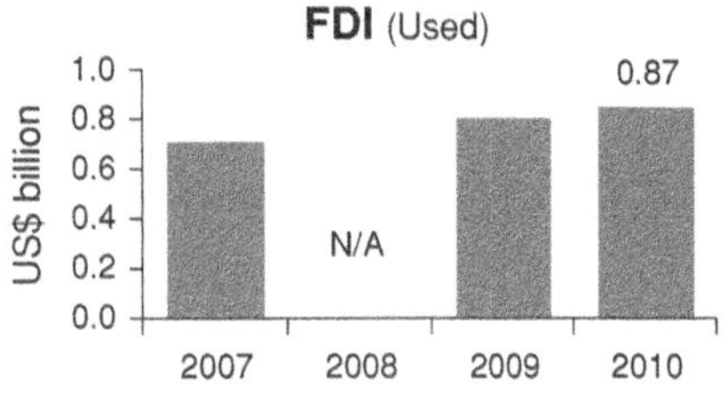

Used FDI was US$0.87 billion in 2010, with 148 new foreign-invested projects.

Changshu by numbers

Item	Unit	2002	2003	2004	2005	2006	2007	2008	2009	2010
Population	m people	1.04	1.04	1.04	1.05	1.06	1.06	1.07	1.10	1.1
GDP	RMBbn	36.50	47.50	56.52	67.88	80.93	97.60	115.00	123.07	145.24
Proportion: primary industry	%	4.40	2.90	2.50	2.40	2.20	1.80	1.70	2.20	2.02
: secondary industry	%	56.60	60.20	60.00	60.70	59.80	59.20	58.30	56.20	56.18
: tertiary industry	%	39.00	36.90	37.50	36.90	38.00	39.00	3.40	41.60	41.8
GDP growth year on year	%	19.00	30.14	18.99	20.10	19.23	20.60	17.83	7.02	18.01
Per capita GDP (all residents)	RMB	35,232	45,761	54,190	64,771	76,711	92,075	107,477	111,882	133,633
Fixed asset investment	RMBbn	12	18	20	23	26	291	32	36	44
Growth year on year	%	65.10	56.58	7.96	19.02	10.81	1,022.98	-89.09	13.59	21.88
Industrial production value	RMBbn	18.95	103.84	130.83	165.03	205.02	256.00	291.83	301.00	365.22
Growth year on year	%	22.00	29.80	26.00	26.90	24.20	24.90	14.00	3.20	3.20
Per capita disposable income of urban residents	RMB	10,268	12,373	15,039	17,203	19,308	22,001	24,602	27,320	30,600
Growth year on year	%	17.80	20.50	21.55	14.39	12.24	13.95	11.82	11.05	12.01
Retail sales	RMBbn	9.75	11.08	12.97	15.10	17.67	21.04	26.37	30.46	36.25
Growth year on year	%	15.10	13.64	17.06	16.42	17.02	19.07	25.33	15.51	19.01
Exports	US$bn	1.35	1.81	2.37	3.23	4.20	6.74	8.68	7.81	11.66
Growth year on year	%	26.40	34.07	30.94	36.29	30.03	60.48	28.78	−10.02	49.30
Imports	US$bn	0.63	0.90	1.61	1.76	2.06	3.89	4.28	3.87	5.67
Growth year on year	%	N/A	42.86	78.89	9.32	17.05	88.83	10.03	−9.58	46.51
Contracted FDI	US$bn	3.24	3.62	3.11	N/A	15.90	1.70	N/A	1.37	2.1
Growth year on year	%	N/A	11.60	N/A	N/A	N/A	6.40	N/A	−14.00	−14.00
Used FDI	US$bn	50.50	101.80	105.20	N/A	N/A	0.71	N/A	0.82	0.87
Growth year on year	%	0.64	101.58	3.34	N/A	N/A	N/A	N/A	N/A	6.10
New FIEs	No	166.00	168.00	188.00	N/A	N/A	245.00	181.00	N/A	N/A
Growth year on year	%	N/A	1.20	11.90	N/A	N/A	N/A	22.50	N/A	N/A

Sources National Bureau of Statistics China Statistical Yearbooks, city government publications, media sources deemed reliable. *N/A* is data not announced in the city government's annual economic and social report and growth data is calculated based on in house data for the previous year. May be available from other sources

Award-Winning Suzhou Satellite City

Kunshan 昆山

In 2010, Kunshan became the first county-level city to achieve a GRP exceeding RMB200 billion.

2.11.1 Spotlight: Development Zone Drivers

The real power behind Kunshan is located in its development zones. The Kunshan New and High Tech Industrial Development Zone (KSND) was the first state-level high-tech zone in China's county-level cities and was promoted to national level in 2010. KSND boasts several essential national-level industrial bases, including a mould manufacturing base and renewable energy (mostly solar and wind energy) base. The zone is also a pioneer nationwide in promoting digital equipment and biopharmaceutical industries, with specific emphasis on robot and siRNA manufacturing.

The Kunshan Economic and Technical Development Zone (KETD) is responsible for 50% of the world's total production of notebook computers (60 million sets in 2009) and is home to several major computer manufacturers from Taiwan, including Acer. While IT accounts for 53% of KETD's industrial structure, precision machinery and daily commodities account for large portions as well (21 and 15% respectively, as of 2010). In the precision machinery industry, major industry players such as Toyota, SANY and Kyokuto have a presence in the zone.

2.12 Economy and Investment

A popular destination for foreign investment, Kunshan has been nicknamed "Little Taipei" in some circles. Investors from Taiwan contributed approximately half of the total FDI volume in the city.

Imports and exports from Kunshan are the sixth highest in the nation (US $82,100 million in 2009) according to the National Bureau of Statistics ranking above major players such as Guangzhou, Tianjin, Ningbo and Qingdao.

The sizable foreign capital inducement, along with the large amount of immigrant residents, has also driven the city's regional demand and greatly contributed to the local development in retail, food and beverage industry, as well as services. Retail sales grew 18.8% year-on-year in 2010

Duke University is developing a 200-acre campus in Kunshan in partnership with the local municipality and Shanghai Jiao Tong University. Kunshan provided 200 acres and funding for the construction of the buildings. The first phase of construction will focus around Duke's Fuqua School of Business and is expected to open in late 2012.

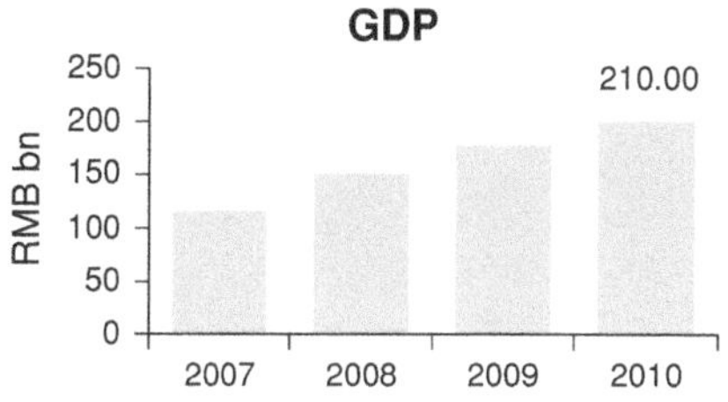

Kunshan's GDP was RMB210 billion in 2010, a 20 percent increase year-on-year.

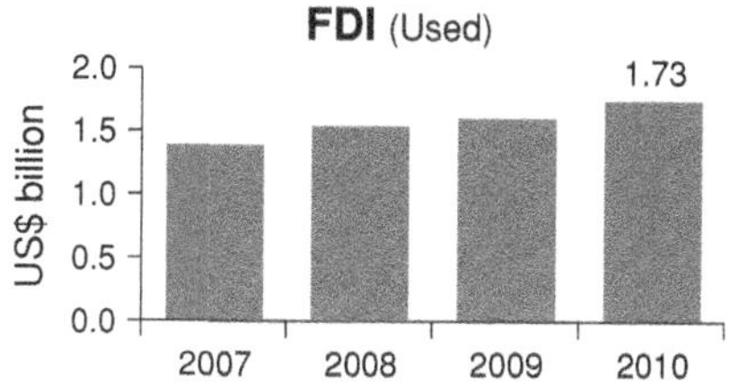

Used FDi was US$1.73 billion in 2010, with 388 new foreign-invested projects that year.

Kunshan by numbers

Item	Unit	2007	2008	2009	2010
Population	m people	0.67	0.69	6.99	7.11
GDP	RMBbn	115.18	150.026	175.01	210.00
Proportion: primary industry	%	N/A	N/A	N/A	N/A
: secondary industry	%	N/A	N/A	N/A	N/A
: tertiary industry	%	N/A	N/A	N/A	N/A
GDP growth year on year	%	20.5	15	16.00	19.99
Per capita GDP (all residents)	RMB	101,000	120,882	135,355	144,500
Fixed asset investment	RMBbn	32,101	37.003	43.00	53.10
Growth year on year	%	14.4	15.3	16.20	23.49
Industrial production value	RMBbn	403.065	500.05	580.32	700.10
Growth year on year	%	30.7	24.1	14.50	20.64
Per capita disposable income of urban residents	RMB	21,927	N/A	27,609	30,923
Growth year on year	%	15.3	N/A	11.30	12.00
Retail sales	RMBbn	16.101	20.187	29.81	35.43
Growth year on year	%	19.3	25.4	16.60	18.85
Exports	US$bn	32.317	38.664	40.76	53.34
Growth year on year	%	32.6	19.6	5.40	30.86
Imports	US$bn	21.118	22.686	21.10	28.79
Growth year on year	%	14.9	7.4	−6.97	36.45
Contracted FDI	US$bn	2.991	3.099	3.15	3.21
Growth year on year	%	19.4	3.6	1.70	1.90
Used FDI	US$bn	1.438	1.603	1.67	1.73
Growth year on year	%	22.7	16.4	3.90	3.59
New FIEs	No	N/A	N/A	N/A	N/A
Growth year on year	%	N/A	N/A	N/A	N/A

Sources National Bureau of Statistics China Statistical Yearbooks, city government publications, media sources deemed reliable. *N/A* is data not announced in the city government's annual economic and social report and may be available from other sources. Growth data is calculated based on in house data for the previous year and may differ from other sources

Suzhou's German-Speaking Little Brother

Taicang 太仓

Taicang is known as a "Hometown of German Enterprises" - more than 130 large German companies such as Siemens have a presence there.

2.13 Infrastructure

2.13.1 Ports and Waterways

Once honored as the "No. 1 Port in the World" in the Yuan Dynasty, Taicang Port it was where Zheng He began his voyages. Today, Taicang Port is considered by the provincial government as the number one foreign trade port in Jiangsu Province.

Taicang Port, which enjoys the same navigation conditions as Shanghai Waigaoqiao Port, is a top-grade port with trunk-line facilities for container transportation. Taicang Port Zone focuses on the development of modern logistics, petrol chemicals, power energy, basic raw materials, among others.

2.14 Economy and Investment

The most striking aspect of Taicang's development is its large GDP over a small population. The city has became one of the more well-developed county-level cities in China with a GDP that is consistently ranked in the top 15 of China's Strongest County-level Cities. Along with the city's port, Taicang's primary industries are manufacturing (specifically precision manufacturing) and hi-tech. In addition to Fortune 500 businesses such as Mobil, Staples, American Standard, Nike and Unilever, Taicang is home to such large domestic businesses as Huaneng, COSCO, Sinochem, China Shipping, CIMC, Sinopec and China Petrol. About a quarter of foreign investment in Taicang comes from the European Union and the United States, with another quarter from Taiwan and about 20% from

Hong Kong, while Japan accounts for about 15%, and Germany and Korea about 5% each (2008).

Taicang is composed of seven towns and o n e development zone: Taicang Economic Development Area. The local government and the TEDA Committee provide special support to small and medium-sized businesses and focus on attracting SMEs. Support is provided in the form of full customs support and small workshops. Furthermore, human resource and business costs are often less than half of those in Shanghai, according to government sources (2010).

According to a report by the German Centre in Shanghai (2009), Taicang is:

- China's largest high-class lubricant producer
- Eastern China's largest LPG base
- Jiangsu province's largest PVC production base
- Asia's largest bike manufacturing base

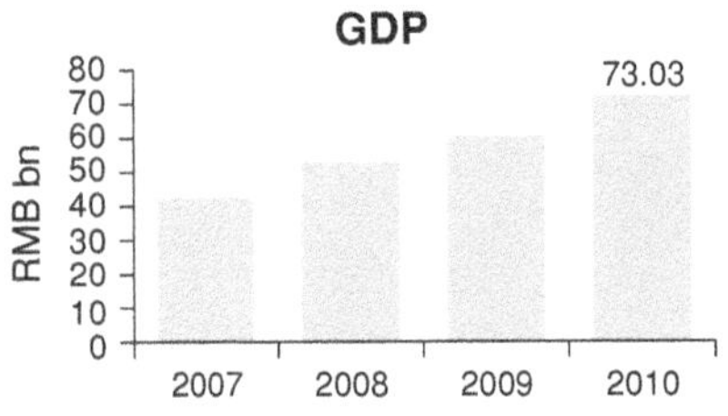

Taicang had a GDP of RMB73.03 billion in 2010, a growth of 2.91 year-on-year.

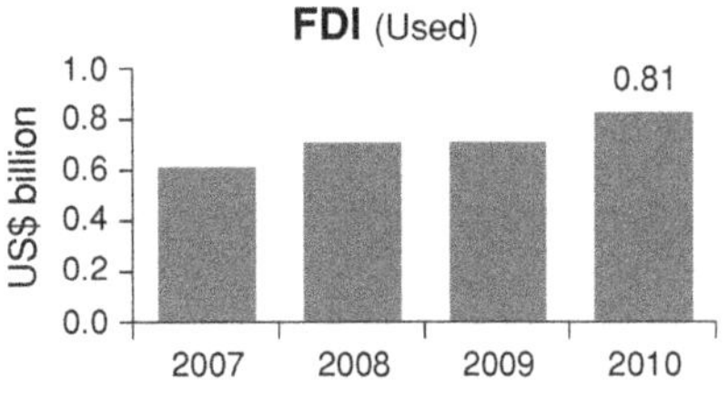

Used FDI was US$0.81 billion in 2010, with 140 new foreign-invested projects.

Taicang by numbers

Item	Unit	2002	2003	2004	2005	2006	2007	2008	2009	2010
Population	m people	0.45	0.45	0.46	0.46	0.46	0.46	0.47	0.67	0.69
GDP	RMBbn	18.01	21.00	24.83	30.00	36.70	44.03	52.80	60.80	73.03
Proportion: primary industry	%	7.10	6.40	5.90	0.05	0.04	3.80	3.50	3.20	3.70
: secondary industry	%	55.80	58.10	60.50	0.60	0.61	60.30	59.60	59.00	57.40
: tertiary industry	%	37.10	35.50	33.60	0.35	0.35	35.90	36.90	37.80	38.90
GDP growth year on year	%	N/A	16.60	18.24	20.82	22.33	19.97	2.79	2.44	2.91
Per capita GDP (all residents)	RMB	40,085	46,667	54,571	65,502	79,783	94,892	113,305	90,476	105,382
Fixed asset investment	RMBbn	6.00	11.12	13.86	17.09	20.10	22.43	24.81	28.43	33.55
Growth year on year	%	37.00	85.33	24.64	23.30	17.61	11.59	10.61	14.59	18.01
Industrial production value	RMBbn	N/A	N/A	N/A	N/A	N/A	110.08	129.62	151.00	190.00
Growth year on year	%	N/A	N/A	N/A	N/A	N/A	22.30	17.75	16.49	25.83
Per capita disposable income of urban residents	RMB	N/A	N/A	14,558	16,700	19,087	21,576	24,624	27,320	30,629
Growth year on year	%	N/A	N/A	N/A	14.71	14.29	13.04	14.13	10.95	12.11
Retail sales	RMBbn	3.21	3.61	4.12	4.70	5.55	6.58	8.19	9.82	14.14
Growth year on year	%	13.40	12.46	14.13	14.08	18.09	18.56	24.47	19.90	43.99
Exports	US$bn	0.93	1.17	1.46	N/A	2.36	3.06	3.89	2.78	4.10
Growth year on year	%	27.40	25.81	24.79	N/A	N/A	29.66	27.12	−28.53	47.48
Imports	US$bn	0.74	1.09	1.42	N/A	N/A	N/A	N/A	2.70	4.60
Growth year on year	%	25.40	47.30	30.28	N/A	N/A	N/A	N/A	N/A	70.37
Contracted FDI	US$bn	0.80	1.22	0.93	0.93	1.20	1.36	1.39	1.41	1.53
Growth year on year	%	35.60	52.50	−23.77	0.00	29.03	13.33	2.21	1.44	8.51
Used FDI	US$bn	0.40	0.62	0.72	0.30	0.45	0.62	0.74	0.75	0.81
Growth year on year	%	60.00	55.00	16.13	−58.33	50.00	37.78	19.35	1.35	8.00
New FIEs	No	223.00	248.00	N/A	N/A	N/A	N/A	N/A	N/A	N/A
Growth year on year	%	43.00	11.20	N/A	N/A	N/A	N/A	N/A	N/A	N/A

Sources National Bureau of Statistics China Statistical Yearbooks, city government publications, media sources deemed reliable. *N/A* is data not announced in the city government's annual economic and social report and may be available from other sources. Growth data is calculated based on in house data for the previous year and may differ from other sources

Wuxi 无锡

Outsourcing and Overseas Entrepreneurs

Wuxi's "530 Plus" Project (2011-2013) aims to attract 30 overseas entrepreneurs in the new energy, medical, IT, new material, advanced manufacturing and environment protection fields.

Traditionally a manufacturing city, Wuxi has recently taken steps to replace its manufacturing focus with a growing service outsourcing industry. This plan aims to attract US $30-40 billion for service outsourcing businesses and create service outsourcing jobs for one million people by 2020.

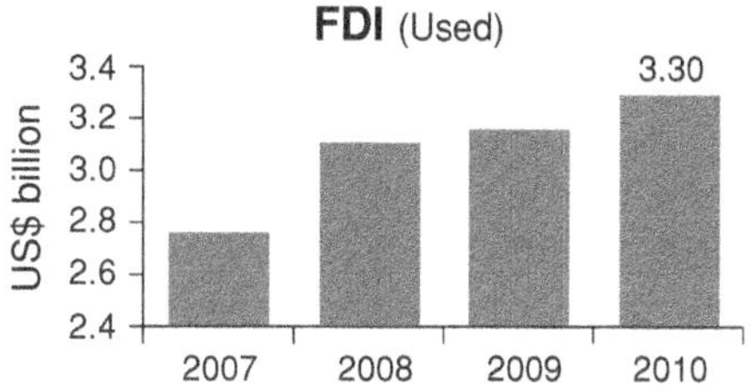

Used FDI was US$3.3 billion in 2010, with 587 new foreign-invested projects. The city has projects from 544 Fortune 500 companies (2010).

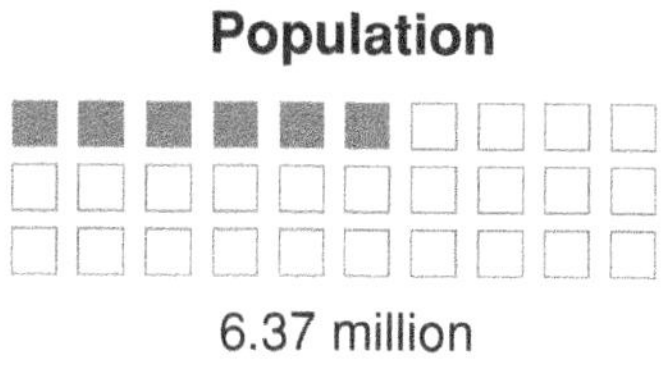

2.15 Infrastructure

2.15.1 Railways

Wuxi is an important transportation hub for Eastern China due to its important geographic location. As of July 2010, Wuxi is connected to the Shanghai–Nanjing high-speed railway, and it now takes about 34 min to go to Shanghai from Wuxi, and only 55 min to Nanjing. Furthermore, with the completion of the Shanghai–Beijing Line in July 2011, Wuxi now has a high-speed link to Beijing. By 2020, Wuxi is expected to have at least seven railway lines.

2.15.2 Ports and Waterways

With the Yangtze, the Grand Canal and the Lake Taihu, Wuxi has seven waterways, totaling 1,656 km. The ocean passenger and cargo transport of Wuxi mainly passes by the Shanghai, Zhangjiagang and Jiangyin ports. Wuxi is 165 km from the port of Shanghai, 43 km away from the port of Zhangjiagang, and 38 km from the port at Jiangyin. Wuxi is one of the 34 main port hubs in China.

2.15.3 Spotlight: Lake Tai

Often referred to as "the pearl of Tai Lake," Wuxi and its residents depend heavily their lake for their water supply. Yet Tai Lake has suffered from major algae blooms and cyanobateria pollution in recent years. After an accident in the spring of 2007, when an algae outbreak contaminated the water supply for 10 days, the State Council put together a plan to clean the lake by 2020. Authorities forced small chemical and manufacturing plants near the lake to close or relocate to northern Jiangsu province, instituted strict monitoring of factory effluents, built sewage treatment facilities and dredged tributary mouths to remove sediments. Media has reported that many long-established companies such as Jiangsu Wuxi Steel and the Wuxi Coke Chemical Factory have shut down their factories along the city's waterways and moved into new development parks.

2.16 Economy and Investment

In order to achieve its targets for the service outsourcing industry, the Wuxi government launched a university graduate training program in 2009, providing rebates to outsourcing companies for hiring a training program graduate, and granted subsidies to program participants upon graduation. As a training base for outsourcing businesses, India's National Institute of Information Technologies (NIIT) currently runs an outsourcing college in Wuxi.

One of Wuxi's key economic development strategies is known as the Wuxi "530" Plan, a program targeted to attract advanced overseas entrepreneurs to the city between 2006 and 2011. Wuxi's 530 Project was extended into the ongoing 530 Plus Project, which aims to attract 30 foreign high-tech entrepreneurs within 2 years (2011–2013), particularly in the fields of new energy, pharmaceutical and medical, IT, new material, advanced manufacturing and environment protection. Targeted foreign entrepreneurs include leaders in their academic or technological field, those with in-demand core technology and those with overseas entrepreneurship experience.

In 2010, 587 new foreign-invested enterprises established themselves in Wuxi and the number of Fortune 500 companies in the city rose to 144, a large number relative to other regional cities. One of these companies is Caterpillar, which has many of its manufacturing and engine R&D projects in the city. The majority of foreign investment into Wuxi has gone into the service industries.

Wuxi defines its eight strategic emerging industries as: new energy, new materials, energy saving, microelectronics, biotechnology and new medicine, software and service outsourcing, industrial design and cultural industries. In 2010, these industries generated RMB 410.37 billion, up by 28.2%.

2.16.1 Resources

Wuxi Government
http://en.wuxi.gov.cn/

Key Industries

- IT and electronics
- Fine chemicals
- Precision machinery
- Metallurgy
- High-grade garments

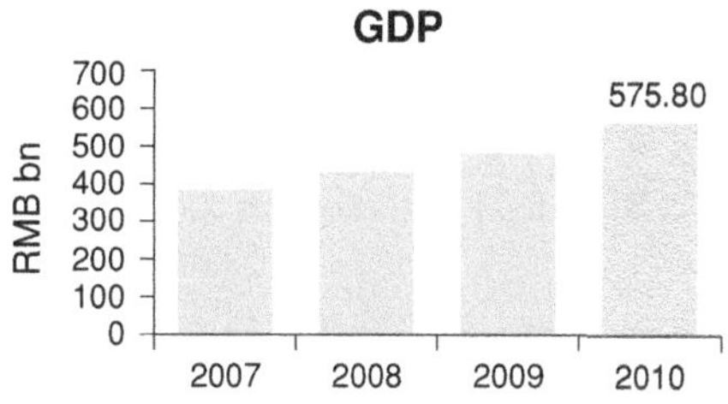

Wuxi's GDP was RMB575.8 billion in 2010, 15 percent growth year-on-year.

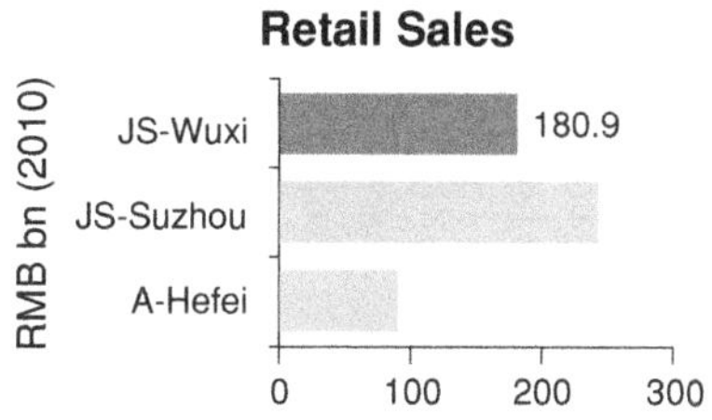

Wuxi's retail sales reached RMB180.9 billion in 2010, quite high (but lower than neighboring Suzhou).

Wuxi by numbers

Item	Unit	2002	2003	2004	2005	2006	2007	2008	2009	2010
Population	m people	4.39	4.43	4.47	4.53	4.58	4.62	6.10	6.20	6.37
GDP	RMBbn	160.20	190.20	235.00	280.50	330.00	385.80	441.90	499.20	575.80
Proportion: primary industry	%	3.60	N/A	2.00	1.30	1.50	N/A	N/A	N/A	1.80
: secondary industry	%	54.90	N/A	57.80	60.90	59.70	N/A	N/A	N/A	55.70
: tertiary industry	%	41.50	39.70	40.20	37.80	38.80	N/A	N/A	N/A	42.50
GDP growth year on year	%	17.79	18.73	23.55	19.36	17.65	16.91	14.54	12.97	15.34
Per capita GDP (all residents)	RMB	36,492	42,935	52,573	61,921	72,052	83,506	72,443	80,516	90,392
Fixed asset investment	RMBbn	53.78	89.33	111.41	133.51	147.49	167.40	187.70	238.76	298.57
Growth year on year	%	16.99	17.65	22.45	17.78	16.36	15.90	−13.25	11.14	12.27
Industrial production value	RMBbn	79.65	99.27	123.14	135.31	166.24	198.42	239.80	265.10	298.60
Growth year on year	%	16.62	24.63	24.05	9.88	22.86	19.36	20.85	10.55	12.64
Per capita disposable income of urban residents	RMB	9,988	11,647	13,588	16,005	18,189	20,898	23,605	25,027	27,750
Growth year on year	%	5.65	16.61	16.67	17.79	13.65	14.89	12.95	6.02	10.88
Retail sales	RMBbn	44.43	48.70	57.92	82.41	95.95	113.48	139.20	165.14	180.90
Growth year on year	%	13.69	9.61	18.93	42.28	16.43	18.27	22.66	18.64	9.54
Exports	US$bn	5.14	7.33	11.02	15.55	21.44	29.32	35.79	26.10	36.27
Growth year on year	%	42.78	42.61	50.34	41.11	37.88	36.75	22.07	−27.07	38.97
Imports	US$bn	4.60	7.05	10.82	13.65	17.74	21.83	20.24	17.93	24.90
Growth year on year	%	49.84	53.26	53.52	26.07	30.04	23.03	−7.28	−11.41	38.87
Contracted FDI	US$bn	2.90	5.01	6.50	7.84	3.28	5.45	5.14	4.10	4.75
Growth year on year	%	−3.33	72.76	29.74	N/A	N/A	66.16	−5.69	−20.23	15.85
Used FDI	US$bn	1.74	2.70	3.30	2.52	2.75	2.77	3.17	3.20	3.30
Growth year on year	%	28.22	55.23	22.18	−23.73	9.34	0.65	14.44	0.95	3.12
New FIEs	No	N/A	N/A	N/A	N/A	N/A	N/A	N/A	N/A	N/A
Growth year on year	%	N/A	N/A	N/A	N/A	N/A	N/A	N/A	N/A	N/A

Sources National Bureau of Statistics China Statistical Yearbooks, city government publications, media sources deemed reliable. *N/A* is data not announced in the city government's annual economic and social report and may be available from other sources. Growth data is calculated based on in house data for the previous year and may differ from other sources

Yangzhou 扬州

Ancient Grand Canal Town, Modern Port City

"Water is the soul of Yangzhou, the Grand Canal the lifeline of Yangzhou, the Yangtze River the mother of Yangzhou," reads a local government development pamphlet.

Until the nineteenth century, Yangzhou was a major national trade center and a transport hub due to its location at the junction of the Yangtze, the Grand Canal and the Huai River. Though its economy started to go into decline in the 1850s, in the past two decades growth has recovered significantly, and today Yangzhou is recognized as one of Jiangsu Province's strongest economies.

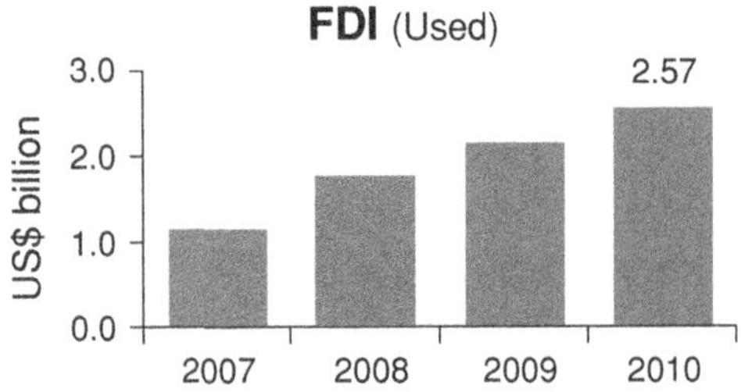

Used FDI was US$2.57 billion in 2010, with 338 new foreign-invested enterprises.

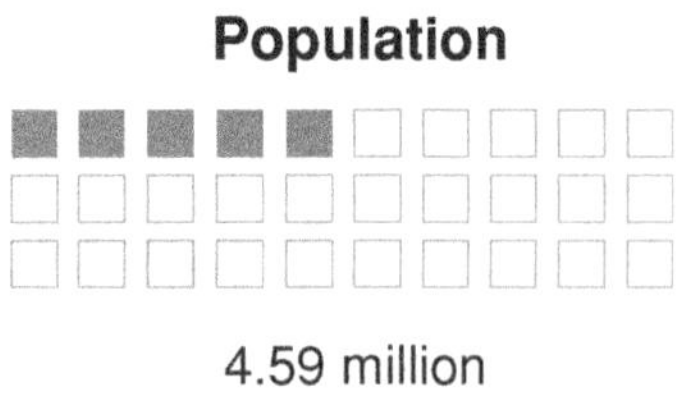

2.17 Infrastructure

2.17.1 Railways

Yangzhou sits on the Taizhou–Nanjing railway line and also provides direct passenger service to Xi'an, Wuhan and Guangzhou. Travel to the east coast is possible by crossing the Zhenjiang–Yangzhou Bridge and taking a train from the Zhenjiang station. In 2011, Yangzhou became linked to the newly operational Beijing–Shanghai high-speed railway. It now takes only about 4 h and 30 min by train to get to Beijing, and about 1 h and 30 min to reach Shanghai.

2.17.2 Ports and Waterways

The Yangzhou Port is the main channel for importing and exporting goods in Yangzhou because it lowers logistics costs. The Yangzhou section of the Beijing–Hangzhou Grand Canal is 143 km long and allows the passage of 1,000 DWT of ships all year round. Goods transported include iron and steel, timber, minerals, coal, grain, cotton, container, products of light industry and machinery. The passenger routes reach Nanjing and Wuhan in the west, and Nantong and Shanghai in the east. In addition, the Yangzhou Port is also a major trading port area that also includes Yizheng Port and Jiangdu Port. Together, these trade areas have an annual throughput of 26 million tons.

2.17.3 Spotlight: Greater Nanjing Cluster

Eight cities of Anhui and Jiangsu provinces, including Yangzhou, signed the "Nanjing Declaration" in July 2011, committing to plans for an urban cluster agglomeration centered around Nanjing. The agglomeration will include transportation development. The major task for the 12th Five-Year Plan (2011–2015) period is to speed up the construction of ten planned rail link and airport projects. The industries to take priority under this plan are high-tech, advanced manufacturing, modern tourism, the cultural industry and urban special agriculture.

2.18 Economy and Investment

Yangzhou has the fifth strongest economy in China, according to China-Business Full City Rankings by the Economist Intelligence Unit in November 2010. The city's foreign trade volume in 2010 stood at US $8.24 billion, of which exports accounted for US $6.05 billion. Yangzhou's major export market is Europe and exports to the EU in 2010 totaled US $1.491 billion, a 11.94% increase year-on-year.

Yangzhou attracted utilized FDI of US $2.57 billion in 2010, increasing 13.2% year-on-year. Leading companies include Siemens, which is establishing a motor production JV; Yangzhou Rongtai Industrial Development Co, known for making aluminum and magnesium die castings; Yangzhou Yaxing Motor Coach, a Shanghai-listed bus manufacturer; Baosheng Group, China's leading producer of wire, cable and other electrical parts; and EMS, the world's biggest manufacturer of metal compound materials. Yangzhou is EMS's sole manufacturing facility in Asia, and will serve its Asian and European markets.

Yangzhou has over 400 large-scale auto and shipbuilding businesses, the industrial output value of which reached RMB 80.1 billion in 2010. Yangzhou's mechanical equipment industry mainly includes plate process equipment and products such as CNC metal-forming equipment, and steel pipes. Yangzhou is located in the middle of the lower Yangtze River chemical industrial region, close to several chemical industrial parks, Jiangsu oilfield and the cross-River station of the East–West Gas Diversion Project pipelines. Yangzhou is seen as a national-level industrial base for smart grids, green new energy sources and a specialty base for photoelectric technologies, including silicon, solar cells and photovoltaic lighting. Semiconductor lighting projects are also big in the city, with the city's LED lighting output accounting for one-ninth of the country's total. In its 12th Five-Year Plan, Yangzhou plans to build "China's optical electric city" with an LED industry valued at over RMB100 billion.

2.18.1 Resources

Yangzhou Government
http://www.yangzhou.gov.cn/

Key Industries

- Petrochemicals
- Automobiles and spare parts
- Electronic information
- Ship machinery
- Textile garments
- Electrical cables
- Medicine & medical instruments
- Metal plate equipment
- Manufacturing

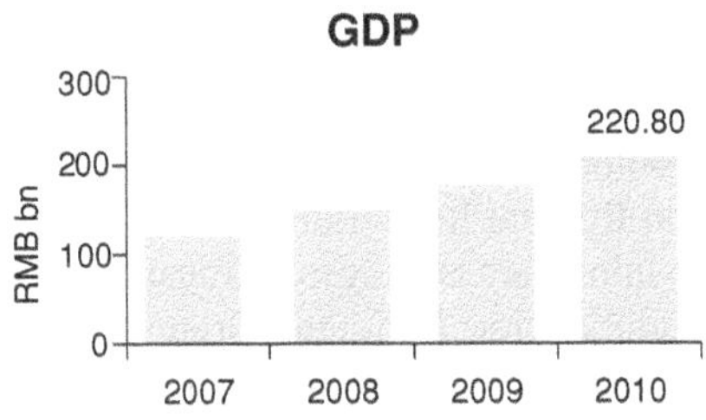

Yangzhou's GDP was RMB220.8 billion in 2010, a 18.9 percent growth year-on-year.

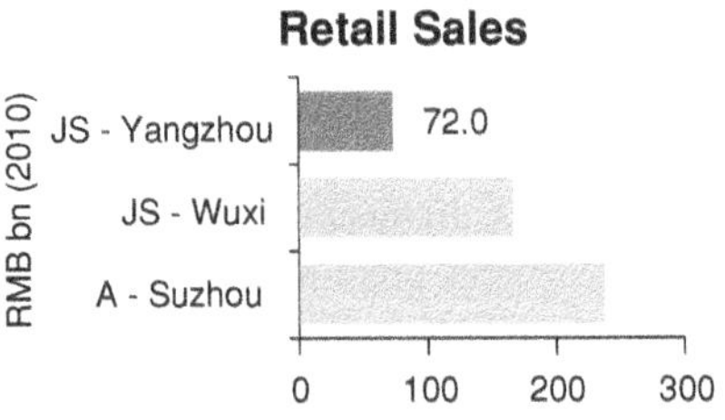

Yangzhou's retail sales reached RMB72 billion in 2010, low compared to neighboring cities.

Yangzhou by numbers

Item	Unit	2002	2003	2004	2005	2006	2007	2008	2009	2010
Population	m people	4.52	4.54	4.544	4.56	4.59	4.59	4.6	4.59	4.59
GDP	RMBbn	55.89	64.72	78.81	92.2	110	131.1	157.33	185.64	220.8
Proportion: primary industry	%	12.7	11.6	10.1	0.093	8.5	7.7	7.47	7.8	7.2
: secondary industry	%	48.8	50.5	53.3	0.562	56.5	57	57.06	56.1	55.7
: tertiary industry	%	38.6	37.9	36.6	0.345	35	35.3	35.47	36.1	37.1
GDP growth year on year	%	9.6	15.8	21.8	17	19.3	19.2	20	18	18.9
Per capita GDP (all residents)	RMB	12,368	14,300	17,315	20,389	24,540	29,400	34,218	41,406	48,955
Fixed asset investment	RMBbn	18.02	24.7	33.01	41	53.33	71.79	95	106.39	133.2
Growth year on year	%	N/A	37.1	33.6	24.2	30.1	34.6	32.3	12	25.2
Industrial production value	RMBbn	23.74	22.65	36.66	38.88	50.03	71.55	90.66	N/A	138.9
Growth year on year	%	N/A	−4.6	61.9	6.1	28.7	43	26.7	N/A	16.1
Per capita disposable income of urban residents	RMB	7,833	8,705	9,851	11,379	12,945	15,057	17,389	19,416	21,766
Growth year on year	%	N/A	11.1	13.2	15.5	13.8	16.3	15.5	11.7	12.1
Retail sales	RMBbn	18.28	19.8	22.8	26.37	35.58	41.89	52.13	61.9	71.95
Growth year on year	%	N/A	8.3	15.2	15.7	34.9	17.7	24.4	18.7	16.2
Exports	US$bn	0.8	1.11	1.35	1.91	2.36	3.25	4.57	4.01	6.06
Growth year on year	%	N/A	38.8	21.6	41.5	23.6	37.7	40.6	−12.3	51.1
Imports	US$bn	0.71	0.91	1.07	0.89	0.91	1.21	1.63	1.42	2.18
Growth year on year	%	N/A	28.2	17.6	−16.8	2.2	33	34.7	−12.9	53.5
Contracted FDI	US$bn	0.51	0.96	1.64	2.43	2.45	3.37	5.01	5.61	N/A
Growth year on year	%	N/A	88.2	70.8	48.2	0.8	37.6	48.7	12	N/A
Used FDI	US$bn	0.26	0.48	0.81	1.25	0.76	1.15	1.72	2.27	2.57
Growth year on year	%	N/A	84.6	68.8	54.3	−39.2	51.3	49.6	32	13.2
New FIEs	No	214	295	330	371	N/A	N/A	N/A	N/A	335
Growth year on year	%	N/A	N/A	N/A	N/A	N/A	N/A	N/A	N/A	N/A

Sources National Bureau of Statistics China Statistical Yearbooks, city government publications, media sources deemed reliable. *N/A* is data not announced in the city government's annual economic and social report and may be available from other sources. Growth data is calculated based on in house data for the previous year and may differ from other sources

ZHEJIANG PROVINCE
浙江省

While neighboring Shanghai aims to become China's financial center, Zhejiang aims to become the SME financial center, with centers in Hangzhou, Ningbo and Wenzhou.

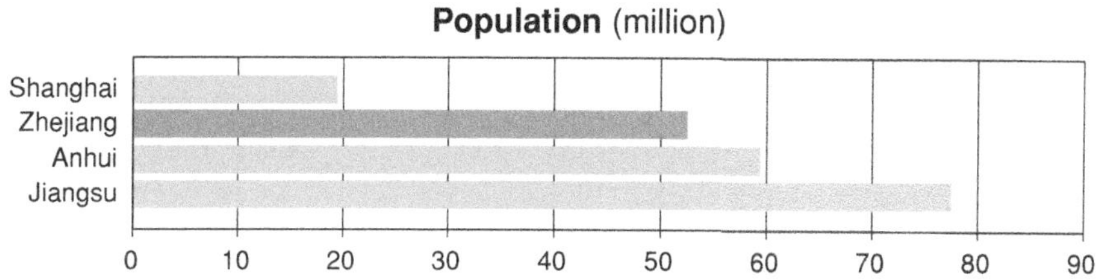

GDP by Industry Level

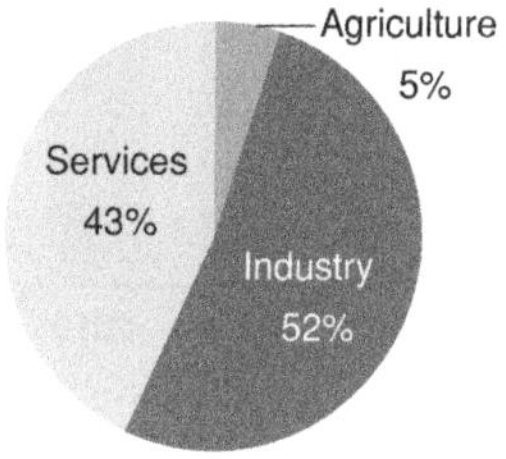

Pillar Industries

- Electromechanical industry
- Textiles
- Chemicals
- Food
- Construction materials

Zhejiang's economic success has been largely home grown, as opposed to being built on support from the central government or huge inflows of FDI. While this is starting to change as multinationals relocate out of Shanghai and into the surrounding regions, the previous absence of outside help has helped to form an entrepreneurial spirit that some dub "the Zhejiang model." This model emphasizes small businesses that are responsive to market fluctuations, large local government investments into public infrastructure and bulk production of low cost goods for both domestic consumption and export.

As such, the provincial capital of Hangzhou has the best business environment in China according to Forbes Magazine (2010), thanks in large part to its fast GDP growth and its business-friendly regulations. The provincial government is working to better connect smaller cities with Hangzhou and in 2011, approved the blueprint for the Hangzhou Urban Economic Circle development project. A joint initiative between four cities in the province (Hangzhou, Huzhou, Jiaxing, Shaoxing), the plan prioritizes transportation infrastructure improvements, including new public bus lines, a trans-city express railway system, and a restructuring plan for the canal to facilitate water transportation.

2.19 Economy

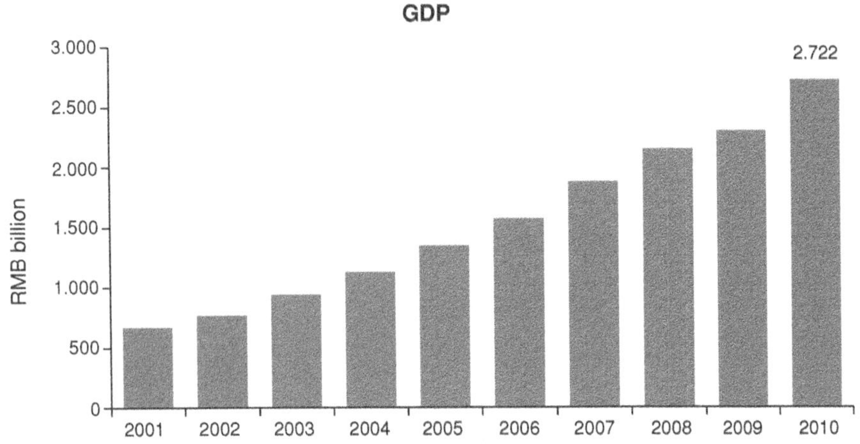

Zhejiang's wealth comes from its manufacturing industry, which is focused in electromechanical industries, textiles, chemical industries, food and construction materials. Over the last 10 years, heavy industries like electric equipment and machinery, raw chemical materials and chemical products have developed rapidly, accounting for more than 50% of the province's industrial output.

Zhejiang's economy was traditionally focused in light industry, but the province has been transitioning towards high potential industries like services, including biomedical services. It is projected that the services sector will account for 48% of Zhejiang's GDP growth rate by 2015.

Zhejiang is targeting an 8% annual GDP growth rate in its 12th Five-Year Plan. Given that annual GDP growth was 11.8% during the 11th Five-Year Plan, this reserved growth rate has drawn the attention of policy watchers. The government has indicated that this conservative growth rate will aid in the continual upgrade and reform of the local economic structure.

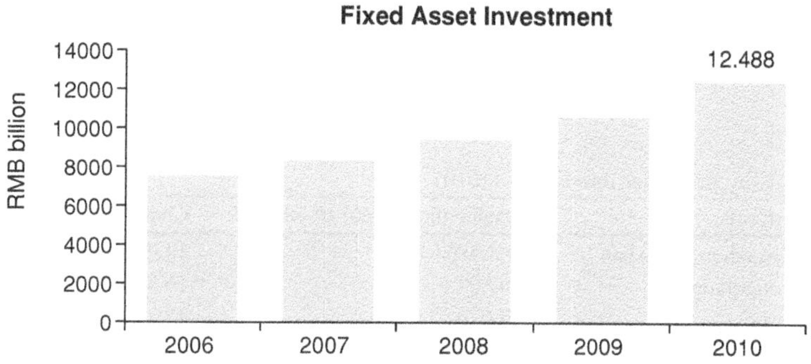

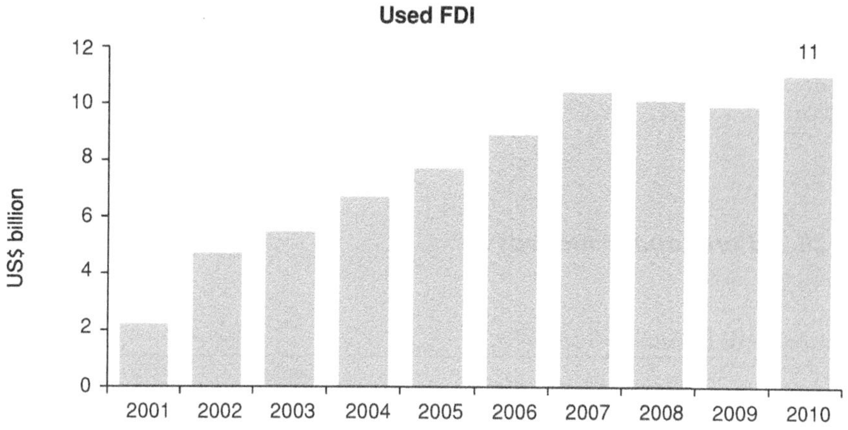

One of the provincial government's major aims in the coming years is to further develop high-tech industries, particularly biotechnology, medicine and new materials. This development will focus on a few important economic belts: Beilun to Ningbo (cities along the Shanghai–Hangzhou–Ningbo Expressway, like Shaoxing, Jiaxing and Huzhou), the coastal cities of Wenzhou and cities along the Zhejiang—Jiangxi and Wenzhou—Taizhou railways.

Zhejiang attracted more than US $11 billion in FDI in 2010, which represents a 10.7% increase year-on-year.

2.20 Infrastructure

2.20.1 Air

Zhejiang's airports by passenger throughput (2010)

City	Airport	Passenger throughput (# people)	Change y-on-y (%)
Hangzhou	Hangzhou Xiaoshan	17,068,585	14.2
Wenzhou	Yongqiang	5,326,802	10.5
Ningbo	Lishe	4,517,070	12
Yiwu	Yiwu	695,148	24.2
Taizhou	Luqiao	616,861	17.1
Zhoushan	Putuo Shan	356,869	−20.3
Quzhou	Quzhou	133,498	4

Source National Airport Throughput Rankings Civil Aviation Administration of China, March 2011

2.20.2 Ports and Waterways

Zhejiang ports by throughput (2010)

Port	Goods		Containers	
	National rank	Throughput (100 million tons)	National rank	Throughput (million TEU)
Sea ports				
Ningbo–Zhoushan	1	6.33	3	1,314.65
River ports				
Huzhou	4	1.44		

Source Transportation via public waterways development statistical report, Ministry of Transport, April 2011

2.20.3 Major Cities (by GDP)

- Hangzhou (Provincial capital)
- Ningbo
- Wenzhou

2.20.4 Resources

Zhejiang Provincial Government
www.zhejiang.gov.cn

Zhejiang Foreign Trade and Economic Cooperation Bureau
www.zftec.gov.cn

Historical Context

Zhejiang was first established as a province during the Ming Dynasty and since then its borders have changed very little. Zhejiang's golden age began in 1100. Hangzhou, the province's present day capital, was also the capital of the Song Dynasty. Renowned for its prosperity and beauty, Hangzhou may have been the largest city in the world at the time with an estimated population of 1 million in 1275. Marco Polo, who visited Hangzhou in the thirteenth century, described the city as the "finest and noblest in the world."

The Taiping Rebellion shook Hangzhou in 1860, destroying the city and decimating its population. Regardless, Hangzhou managed to build its way back up to its former reputation of luxury and opulence.

Zhejiang received a lot of attention during the twentieth century. In the late 1920s, the province became a base of power for the Nationalist Party of Chiang Kai-shek and subsequently the Zhejiang elite soon came to dominate the nationalist regime. After the communists took control in 1949, the government established a rival Zhejiang provincial government that lasted until 1955.

Although southern Zhejiang is not suitable for farming and was traditionally underdeveloped, hard work and low labor costs have transformed the area into a major export hub. The success of the south together with the historical wealth of the north has allowed Zhejiang to become one of the richest provinces in China.

Zhejiang by numbers

	Unit	2002	2003	2004	2005	2006	2007	2008	2009	2010
Population	m people	46.7	46.8	47.2	46	46.3	46.6	46.9	47.2	52
GDP	RMBbn	767	939.5	1,124.30	1,341.80	1,571.80	1,875.40	2,146.30	2,299.00	2,722.7
Proportion: primary industry	%	8.8	7.8	7.3	6.1	5.7	4.9	4.6	4.8	5
: secondary industry	%	51.2	52.5	53.7	46.6	45.6	45.4	47.3	50.3	51.9
: tertiary industry	%	40	39.7	39	34.2	34.1	33.5	35.5	38.3	43.1
GDP growth year on year	%	12.3	13.2	14.3	15.2	17.1	19.3	14.4	7.1	11.8
Per capita GDP (all residents)	RMB	16,570	19,730	23,942	27,661	31,825	37,358	42,166	44,641	52,059
Fixed asset investment	RMBbn	345.8	494.7	594.5	669.6	759.3	842	932.3	1,074.20	1,248.8
Growth year on year	%	24.9	38.1	20.2	10.5	13.4	10.9	10.7	15.2	16.3
Industrial production value	RMBbn	352.4	431	538.1	634.3	758.5	909	1,032.90	1,051.80	1,039.7
Growth year on year	%	13.5	16.4	17	17.9	19.6	19.8	13.6	1.8	16.2
Per capita disposable income of urban residents	RMB	11,716	13,180	14,546	16,294	18,265	20,574	22,727	24,611	27,359
Growth year on year	%	13.4	12.5	7.4	12	12.1	12.6	10.5	8.3	7
Retail sales	RMBbn	287.9	315.7	364.5	464.6	535.8	627.1	753.3	862.2	1016.3
Growth year on year	%	12.6	10.9	15.5	14.5	15.3	17	20.1	14.5	19
Exports	US$bn	29.42	41.6	58.2	76.8	100.9	128.3	154.2	133	180.5
Growth year on year	%	28	41.5	39.8	32	31.4	27.2	20.2	−13.7	35.7
Imports	US$bn	12.5	19.82	27.07	30.6	38.2	48.6	56.9	54.7	73
Growth year on year	%	27.7	58	36.6	13.3	24.8	27.2	17.1	−3.9	33.4
Contracted FDI	US$bn	7.21	12.1	14.6	16.1	19.1	20.4	17.8	16	20.04
Growth year on year	%	0.5	77.5	20.8	10.3	18.6	6.8	−12.7	−10.1	25.2
Used FDI	US$bn	4.7	5.45	6.7	7.7	8.9	10.4	10.1	9.9	11
Growth year on year	%	3.9	72.4	22.6	14.9	15.6	16.9	−2.9	−1.6	10.7
New FIEs	No	3,364	4,442	3,824	3,396	3,583	2,919	1,858	1,216	1,944
Growth year on year	%	45.6	32.1	−13.9	−11.2	5.5	−18.5	−36.3	−34.6	11.9

Hangzhou 杭州

Zhejiang's Capital City

Forbes Magazine rated the city as having the best business environment in China (2010) thanks to its high living standards, well-developed infrastructure and business friendly regulations.

Best known for its beautiful West Lake and silk industry, Hangzhou is the political, economic and cultural center of Zhejiang province and accounts for nearly a quarter of provincial economic output. Investors choose Hangzhou for a variety of reasons, including lower office set up costs, competitive government tax incentives and a strong network of local IT companies.

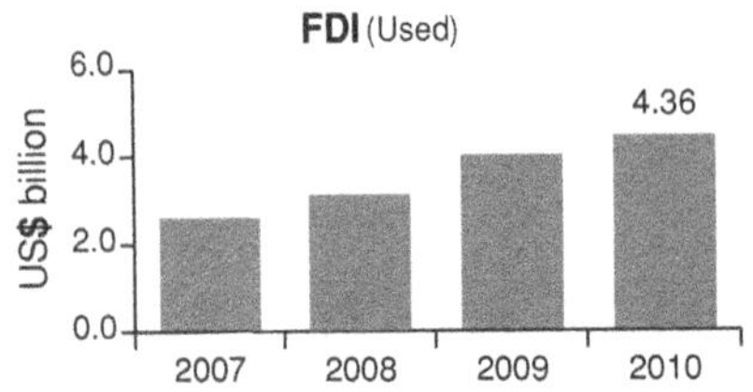

Used FDI was US$4.36 billion, with US$2.2 billion in the service industry and US$1.8 in manufacturing.

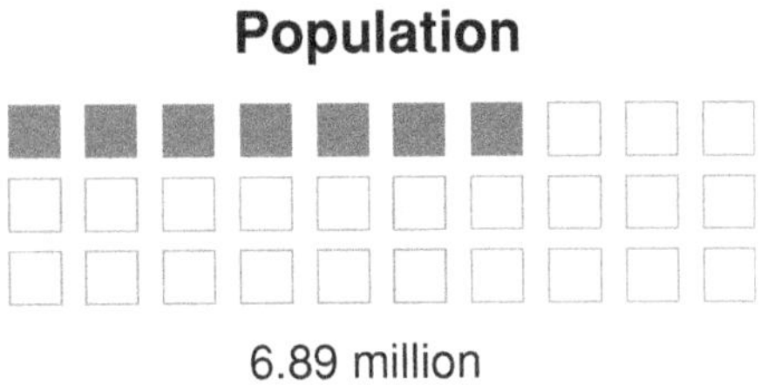

2.21 Infrastructure

The blueprint for the Hangzhou Urban Economic Circle, a major regional economic development project prioritizing transportation infrastructure improvements, was approved in 2011 as a joint initiative between four cities in Zhejiang Province (Hangzhou, Huzhou, Jiaxing, Shaoxing).

2.21.1 Railways

Hangzhou is an important rail transportation hub of east China. Shanghai–Hangzhou, Zhejiang–Jiangxi, Xiaoshan–Ningbo and Xuanchen–Hangzhou railways intersect here. Hangzhou is currently constructing its metro system and is expected to be completed by 2012.

2.21.2 Ports and Waterways

Shanghai and Ningbo's seaports can be reached in around one and a half to two hours. The Beijing–Hangzhou Grand Canal and the Qiantang River are also in close proximity.

2.22 Economy and Investment

Zhejiang province is known for its private enterprises and its capital is no exception. The proportion of non-public economy reached 66% in 2010, up by 1.5% year-on-year.

Industry-wise, Hangzhou has made a name for itself in information technology, software development, telecommunications equipment and electronics. Other major industries include biological medicine, machinery and household appliances and food and beverages.

By the end of 2010, a total of 82 Fortune 500 companies had projects in Hangzhou. Of the 599 foreign-invested enterprises, 200 are non-trade enterprises. Toshiba has set up a global production base and Matsushita invested US $240 million in its largest production base for home electrical appliances in China. China's largest food and beverage company, Wahaha, is headquartered in Hangzhou.

East of downtown, the Hangzhou Economic Development Area's (HEDA) export-oriented manufacturing park is one of the largest production bases for mobile telecommunications equipment in China.

Hangzhou aims to be a major center for research and development by utilizing its strong higher education resources. There are six higher education districts in the city and 37 higher educational institutions, such as Zhejiang University (see spotlight). The Xiasha High Education Park, located in the Hangzhou Economic and Technology Development Area, includes 15 higher education colleges. Some of the key subjects include electronic information engineering, computer science and technology, and manufacturing and automation.

Hangzhou is also a major retail center, with sales of social consumer goods increasing 19% year-on-year in 2010 to reach RMB 214.608 billion. By industry, sale of social consumer goods are approximately 88% of wholesale and retail trade sales and 12% of accommodations and catering industries.

2.22.1 Spotlight: Zhejiang University, #3 in China

Zhejiang University, founded in 1897, is one of the oldest institutions of higher learning and ranks third among all Chinese universities (behind only Beijing's Peking and Qinghua Universities). It is particularly well known for its strength in the sciences—14 faculty members are from the Chinese Academy of Sciences and 12 from the Academy of Engineering. The university is also home to three national engineering and technology research centers: Applied Power Electronic Technology, Optical Instrumentation, and Electrohydraulic Control.

2.22.2 Resources

Hangzhou City Government
http://eng.hangzhou.gov.cn/

Hangzhou Economic and Technical Development Area
http://www.heda.gov.cn/

Key Industries

- Information Technology
- Software Development
- Telecommunications Equipment
- Electronics

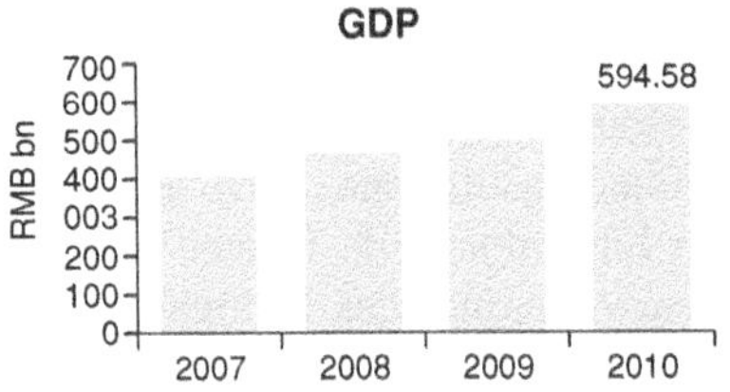

Hangzhou's GDP was RMB594.58 billion in 2010, a 12 percent growth year-on-year.

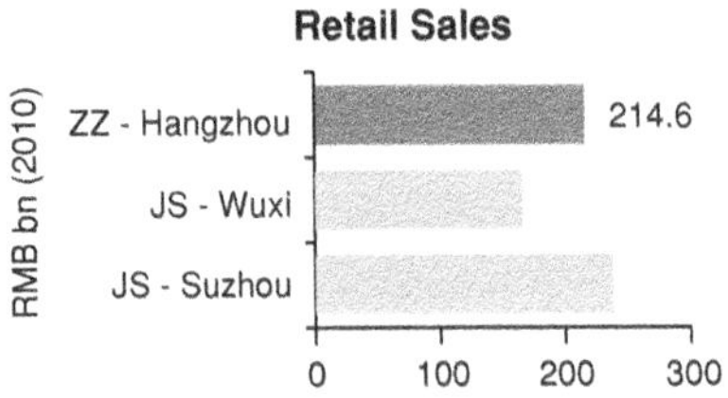

Hangzhou's retail sales reached RMB214.6 billion in 2010, high (but less than neighboring Suzhou).

Hangzhou by numbers

Item	Unit	2002	2003	2004	2005	2006	2007	2008	2009	2010
Population	m people	6.37	6.43	6.52	6.6	6.66	7.86	7.96	8.1	6.89
GDP	RMBbn	178	209.2	251.5	294.27	344.1	410.39	478.12	509.87	594.58
Proportion: primary industry	%	6.3	6.1	5.5	0.05	4.5	4.1	3.7	3.7	3.5
: secondary industry	%	50.7	51.6	53	50.9	50.6	50.2	50	47.8	47.8
: tertiary industry	%	43	42.3	41.5	44.1	44.9	45.7	46.3	48.5	48.7
GDP growth year on year	%	13.2	15	15	13	14.3	14.6	16.5	10	12
Per capita GDP (all residents)	RMB	28,000	32,700	38,858	44,853	51,871	61,313	60,414	74,924	86,281
Fixed asset investment	RMBbn	76.94	100.62	120.52	127.78	146.05	168.41	196.17	229.17	275.31
Growth year on year	%	21.9	30.7	19.7	15.3	10.1	15.3	16.5	15.7	20.1
Industrial production value	RMBbn	77.3	93.5	117.5	132.96	157.15	187.79	N/A	1,064.8	12,821.9
Growth year on year	%	13.7	19.9	18.6	11.3	14.6	19.5	N/A	1.5	19.6
Per capita disposable income of urban residents	RMB	11,778	12,898	14,565	16,601	19,027	21,689	24,104	26,864	30,035
Growth year on year	%	8.1	9.5	12.9	14	14.6	14	11.1	11.5	11.8
Retail sales	RMBbn	52.35	58.75	70.43	97.54	111.24	129.63	155.8	189.40	214.61
Growth year on year	%	14.1	12.4	15.2	14	14	16.5	20	15.8	19.9
Exports	US$bn	8.48	10.95	15.18	19.8	26.23	29.97	33.61	27.18	35.34
Growth year on year	%	16.4	29.2	38.6	30.5	32.4	14.3	12.2	−19.1	30
Imports	US$bn	4.63	7.28	9.32	10.1	12.68	13.46	14.45	13.24	17.02
Growth year on year	%	15.2	57.5	28	8	26	6.2	7.4	−8.4	28.6
Contracted FDI	US$bn	1.7	1.59	3.1	4.01	5.38	5.58	6.23	6.97	7.71
Growth year on year	%	64.6	−6.3	94.5	30.1	34.3	3.7	11.6	11.8	10.7
Used FDI	US$bn	0.65	1.01	1.4	1.71	2.26	2.8	3.31	4.014	4.36
Growth year on year	%	29.2	93.3	39.8	21.5	31.7	24.2	18.2	21.2	8.5
New FIEs	No	587	869	802	756	747	574	483	N/A	599
Growth year on year	%	21.5	48	−7.7	−5.7	−1.2	−23.2	−15.9	N/A	N/A

Sources National Bureau of Statistics China Statistical Yearbooks, city government publications, media sources deemed reliable. *N/A* is data not announced in the city government's annual economic and social report and growth data is calculated based on in house data for the previous year. May be available from other sources

Ningbo 宁波

Zhejiang's Deepwater Port

Ningbo-Zhoushan Port is the largest general cargo port in China, surpassing Shanghai Port (2010), and ranks third in terms of annual throughput

The 12th Five-Year Plan (2011–2016) of Zhejiang province defines Ningbo as the "economic center of South YRD." Government goals in this plan for the city include transforming it into a major base for advanced manufacturing, modern logistics, energy and raw material and a center for shipping finance. The latter goal is based on Ningbo's excellent natural deepwater port, unique among nearby cities.

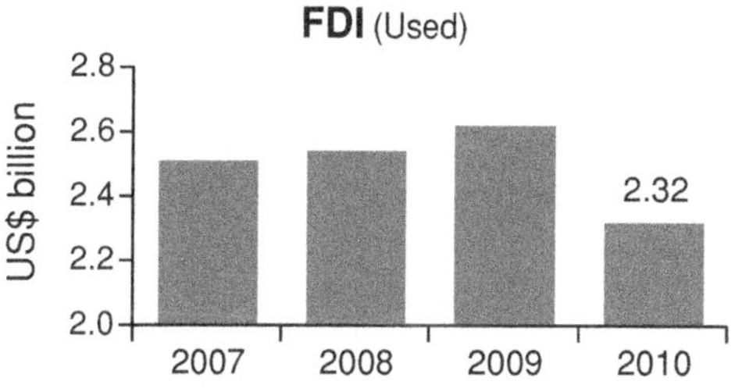

Used FDI was US$2.32 billion in 2010, with 174 new foreign-invested enterprises.

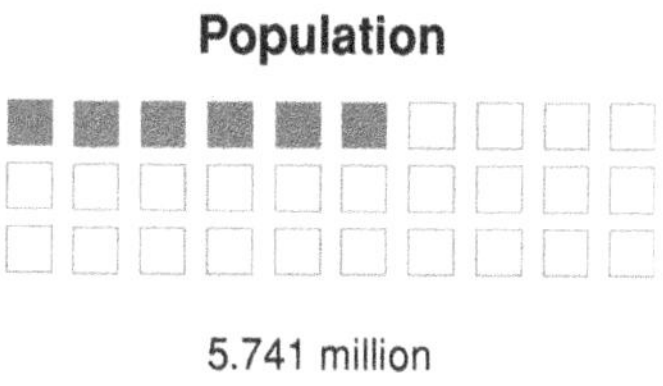

2.23 Infrastructure

Ningbo's construction industry has developed rapidly, with a total production value of RMB 142.51 billion in 2010, an increase of 32.2% year-on-year.

2.23.1 Railways

Ningbo is three to 4 h from Shanghai by rail, with close connections to major cities in China. The Xiao Yong Railroad (connecting Hangzhou and Ningbo) and the Yong Tai Wen Railroad (connecting Ningbo and Wenzhou) are the main railroads in Ningbo. The Hu Hang Yong passenger line (connecting Shanghai, Hangzhou and Ningbo) is under construction. Upon completion, the travel time from Ningbo to Hangzhou will be shortened to 40 min, and the trip from Ningbo to Shanghai will be shortened to 1.5 h.

2.23.2 Ports and Waterways

In 2006, Ningbo Port and Zhoushan Port officially joined together to become Ningbo–Zhoushan Port. In 2010, Ningbo–Zhoushan Port saw its cargo throughput reach over 13 million TEUs, up 25.2% year-on-year. Ningbo–Zhoushan Port is the largest general cargo port in China, with throughput of 629 million tons in 2010, up 8.90% year-on-year. Ningbo Port has the largest number of deepwater berths and receives the most 100,000 DWT vessels in China (2010).

2.24 Economy and Investment

The Ningbo city government's General Plan (2006–2020) envisions the city as "the economic center of the YRD's southern wing" and "Southeast China's port city." Over the next ten years (2010–2020), Ningbo plans to construct a "Smart City" by establishing intelligent application systems, industrial bases and infrastructure, investing RMB 500 million a year. Ningbo was ranked eighth on the Forbes Magazine "Best Cities for Business in Mainland China" (2010).

As such, Ningbo experienced a huge uptake in foreign-funded projects between 2009 and the end of 2010, mostly due to a greater number of large-scale projects. There were 13,336 foreign invested enterprises in Ningbo by the end of 2010. Scale of investment averaged US $10.45 billion in 2010, up 130% year-on-year and projects included ten valued at over US $50 million, mostly in the property sector. Most foreign investment was made in the property market, wholesale and retail businesses, computer services, software, science and technology research, technical assistance and geological exploration.

Home of the famous "Hong Bang" style tailors, Ningbo has a major national presence in garment production and home electric appliance manufacturing. Autoparts, mould and stationary production in the city are also significant. In May 2011, Shanghai Volkswagen Automotive Co., Ltd. announced plans to launch its sixth Chinese auto production plant in Ningbo. Strategic new industries in the city include new materials, new energy, environmental protection, and medical equipment—by 2015, these industries aim to have an industrial output value of RMB 60 billion, accounting for 15% of GDP.

Port development goals by 2015 include container throughput of 20 million TEUs, as well as further developing cooperation with Jiaxing, Wenzhou, Taizhou and other ports. Ningbo's 12th Five-Year Plan emphasized the importance of port development to the local government through emphasizing "soft power to enhance port competitiveness". The government's plans include building a national training base for port logistics and using science, education, research and innovation to enhance the capacity of the port and actively promoting port museums, cultural festivals held in the port, port management training classes and other activities to enhance the international reputation of the port. The city aims to become a commodities trading center and "an influential national and even global trading platform," with turnover of RMB 400 billion by 2015.

Goals for strengthening Ningbo's financial system include an SME focus, specifically expanding loans and financing channels available to SMEs. By 2015, the city also aims to form 1,000 corporate R&D institutions, establish more than 2,500 invention patents and increase R&D expenditures to reach 2.5% of GDP.

2.24.1 Resources

Ningbo Government
http://english.ningbo.gov.cn/

Ningbo Foreign Investment Development Board
http://www.ningbochina.com/en/index.html

Ningbo Economic and Technical Dev. Zone
http://www.netd.gov.cn/en/nbjj_en_gs.php

Ningbo Port Co. Ltd.
http://www.nbport.com.cn/portal/wps/portal/en

Key Industries

- Petrochemicals
- Steel
- Shipbuilding
- Equipment manufacturing
- Automobile and parts
- Textiles
- Non-ferrous metals
- Electronics and Telecommunication

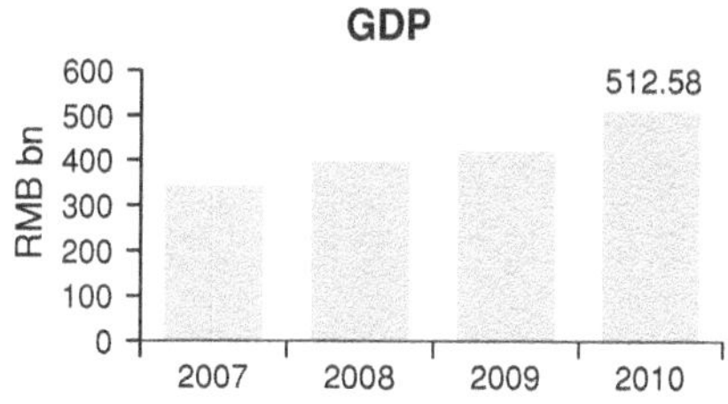

Ningbo's GDP reached RMB512.58 billion in 2010, up 12.4 percent year-on-year.

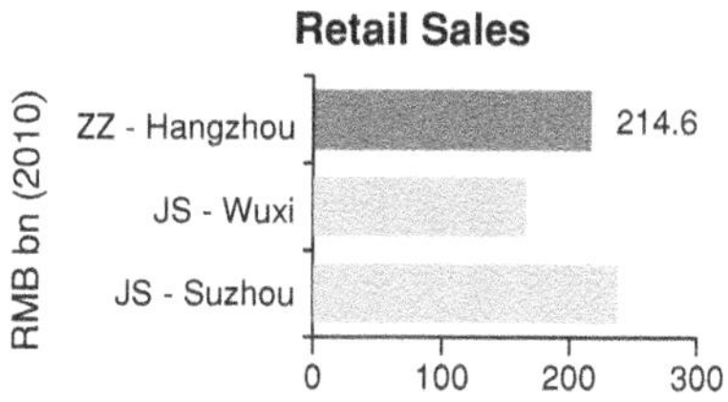

Ningbo's retail sales reached RMB146 billion in 2010, approximately that of neighboring Wenzhou.

Ningbo by numbers

Item	Unit	2002	2003	2004	2005	2006	2007	2008	2009	2010
Population	m people	5.462	5.49	5.53	5.57	5.6	5.67	5.68	5.7	5.741
GDP	RMBbn	150.03	176.99	215.8	244.64	286.45	343.31	396.4	421.46	512.58
Proportion: primary industry	%	7	6.3	0.057	5.3	4.9	N/A	4.2	4.4	4.2
: secondary industry	%	55.2	56.9	0.57	55.3	55	N/A	55.4	53.3	55.6
: tertiary industry	%	37.8	36.8	0.373	39.4	40.1	40.5	40.4	42.3	40.2
GDP growth year on year	%	13.2	18	21.9	13.4	17.1	19.8	15.5	6.3	12.4
Per capita GDP (all residents)	RMB	27,468	32,239	39,024	43,921	51,152	60,549	69,789	73,940	68,162
Fixed asset investment	RMBbn	60.13	83.76	109.57	137.04	154.3	159.79	172.8	200.42	220.65
Growth year on year	%	27.9	39.3	30.8	25.1	12.6	3.6	8.1	16	10.1
Industrial production value	RMBbn	74.95	91.01	108.68	137.04	142.14	176.68	201.23	103	131.712
Growth year on year	%	15	21.4	19.4	26.1	3.7	24.3	13.9	−1.6	32.5
Per capita disposable income of urban residents	RMB	12,970	14,277	15,882	17,408	19,674	22,307	25,304	27,368	30,166
Growth year on year	%	18.8	10.1	11.2	9.6	13	13.4	13.4	8.2	10.2
Retail sales	RMBbn	46.29	52.15	59.56	75.98	88.25	103.55	123.8	143.44	146.04
Growth year on year	%	11.8	12.7	14.2	27.6	16.1	17.3	19.6	15.9	19.9
Exports	US$bn	8.16	12.07	16.69	22.23	28.77	38.3	46.33	38.65	51.97
Growth year on year	%	30.7	47.9	38.3	33.2	29.4	33.0	21.1	−16.6	34.5
Imports	US$bn	4.11	6.74	9.42	11.26	13.44	18.2	21.51	22.16	30.93
Growth year on year	%	55.4	64	39.8	19.5	19.4	35.7	17.9	3.0	39.6
Contracted FDI	US$bn	3.2	3.44	4.14	4.21	4.43	4.5	4.12	3.42	4.05
Growth year on year	%	64	7.5	20.3	1.7	5.2	1.6	−8.4	−17	18.2
Used FDI	US$bn	1.25	1.73	2.1	2.31	2.43	2.51	2.54	2.62	2.32
Growth year on year	%	43	38.4	21.4	10	5.2	3.3	1.2	3.1	−11.5
New FIEs	No	1,017	1,209	1,081	N/A	N/A	N/A	332	177	175
Growth year on year	%	26	18.9	−10.6	N/A	N/A	N/A	N/A	−46.7	−1.3

Sources National Bureau of Statistics China Statistical Yearbooks, city government publications, media sources deemed reliable. *N/A* is data not announced in the city government's annual economic and social report and growth data is calculated based on in house data for the previous year. May be available from other sources

Wenzhou 温州

Home of China's Market Economy

The strength and vitality of Wenzhou's consumer market ranks second in China, after only Guangzhou, according to The Economist Intelligence Unit (Nov, 2010)

Wenzhou claims to be the "first city in China to launch a market economy." While this may or may not be true, small scale market economy is thriving in the city. Individual industrial households still account for 78% of enterprises in the city, while private enterprises account for 19%—foreign-funded enterprises and state-owned enterprises are few and far between.

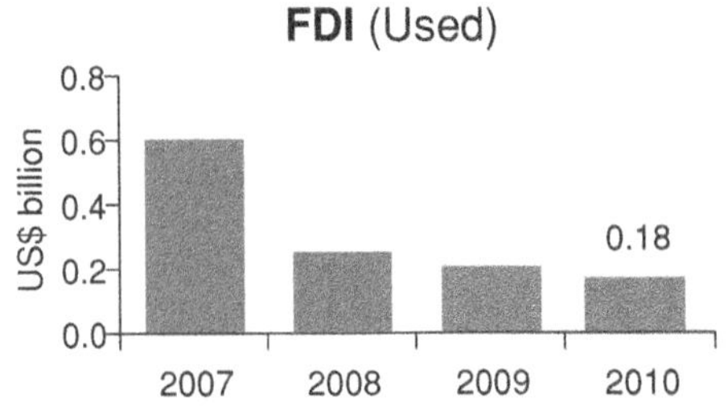

Used FDI was US$0.18 billion in 2010, with 25 new foreign-invested enterprises.

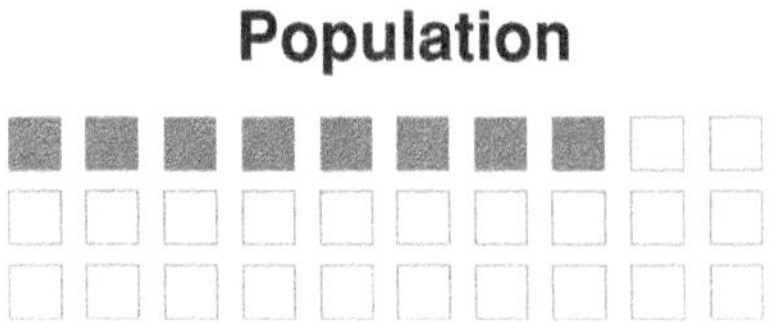

7.87 million

2.25 Infrastructure

Road and water ways are the key methods of transportation of goods in Wenzhou, with the former accounting for approximately 68% of tons of goods transported and the later accounting for 29% (2010).

2.25.1 Ports and Waterways

As of 2010, there are 232 productive berths, including 15 berths with a capacity of over 10,000 tons. Wenzhou Port is in the process of opening international container shipping routes, attracting 15 of the world's top 20 shipping companies.

Goals for the port by 2015 include:

- 1 million tons general cargo throughput
- 100 million TEUs container throughput
- 1.6 million tons total water transportation capacity

2.25.2 Spotlight: Wenzhou's Exports

Wenzhou's harbors allow the mooring of huge cargo ships opening a gateway for export and import commerce in Zhejiang. Major exports are mechanical equipment, synthetic grass, eyeglasses and lighters. Europe is Wenzhou's largest export market.

Exports by region (2010)

Destination	Amount (RMB 100 billion)	%
Europe	59.57	41
Asia	40.24	28
North America	19.07	13
Latin America	13.31	9
Africa	10.86	7
Oceania	2.23	2

The city has been somewhat of a pioneer in utilizing marketing mechanisms to develop urban constructions. Major recently completed construction projects include:

- Zhejiang Yueqing Power Plant (Phase II)
- Multi-purpose Lingkun Port Terminal (Phase I)
- Emperor Ping Wind Farm Projects

Major ongoing construction projects include:

- A power station with capacity of 220 kV
- Construction of Wenzhou private economy Technology Park

2.26 Economy and Investment

After the Chinese government's reform and opening-up policies, Wenzhou became the first city to issue "individual business licenses" (1980) and the fist city to release local regulations on private enterprises (1987).

The city's six key industries—electrical machinery and equipment manufacturing, leather and fur feathers (down), general equipment manufacturing, electricity and heat production, plastic products, and textiles—accounted for 85.5% of industrial output value.

Since around 2000, Wenzhou has become widely known for the large number of property speculators but the government hopes to encourage private equity to enter channels other than property, coal and stocks. The Wenzhou Venture Capital Research Institute, formed by Wenzhou Municipal Government, China Venture Capital Research Institute and Zhejiang Industry & Trade Vocational College, was established in 2010. The aim of the institute is to act as an "incubator" to promote the flow of private capital into the 20–50 top private equity/venture capital funds to be invested in "high-tech enterprises and innovative companies with convincing performances." The head of the institute estimated the city has private capital over RMB 600 billion (US $87.90 billion).

2.26.1 Resources

Wenzhou Government
http://www.wenzhou.gov.cn/

Key Industries

- Electrical machinery and equipment manufacturing
- Leather and fur feathers (down)
- General equipment manufacturing
- Electricity and heat production
- Plastic products
- Textiles

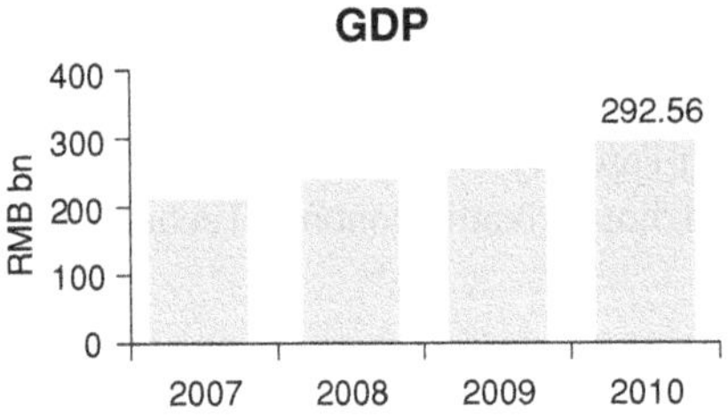

Wenzhou's GDP was RMB292.56 in 2010, a 15.7 percent growth year-on-year.

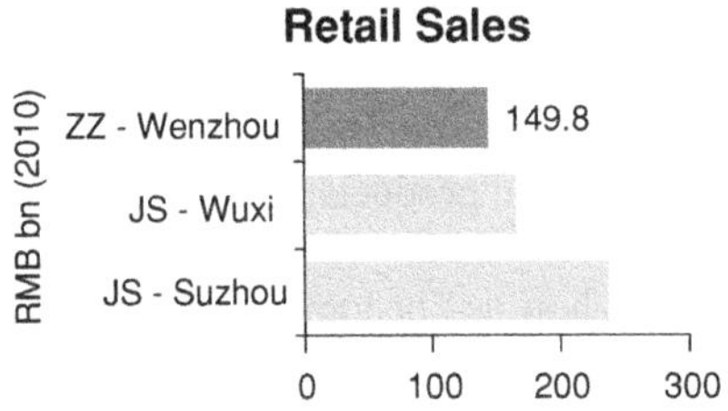

New Fortune 500 Enterprises (2010): 7

Wenzhou by numbers

Item	Unit	2002	2003	2004	2005	2006	2007	2008	2009	2010
Population	m people	7.39	7.42	7.46	7.5	7.56	7.65	7.72	7.79	7.87
GDP	RMBbn	105.5	122	140.26	160	183.44	215.7	242.43	252.79	292.56
Proportion: primary industry	%	5.3	4.7	4.6	4.1	3.5	3.3	3.1	3.2	3.2
: secondary industry	%	56.7	57.2	56.8	54.3	54.7	54.2	53.1	50.9	52.4
: tertiary industry	%	38	38.1	38.6	41.6	41.8	42.5	43.8	45.9	44.4
GDP growth year on year	%	13	15.6	15.0	14.1	14.7	17.6	12.4	4.3	15.7
Per capita GDP (all residents)	RMB	14,217	16,475	18,846	21,384	24,349	28,362	31,555	32,595	37,366
Fixed asset investment	RMBbn	38.78	44.86	50.73	54.2	64.56	73.7	75.84	83.78	93.03
Growth year on year	%	18	15.7	13.1	6.8	19.1	14.2	2.9	10.5	11.0
Industrial production value	RMBbn	52.45	63.16	72.15	79.48	91.59	106.33	117.03	116.37	138.93
Growth year on year	%	13.1	20.4	14.2	10.2	15.2	16.1	10.1	-0.6	19.4
Per capita disposable income of urban residents	RMB	14,591	16,035	17,727	19,805	21,716	24,002	26,172	28,021	31,201
Growth year on year	%	10.5	9.9	10.6	11.7	9.6	10.5	9.0	7.1	11.3
Retail sales	RMBbn	49.1	52.25	58.79	68.1	77.92	90.6	108.3	126.47	149.81
Growth year on year	%	12	6.4	12.5	15.8	14.4	16.3	19.5	16.8	18.5
Exports	US$bn	2.65	3.42	4.58	6.18	8.1	10.1	11.9	10.93	14.54
Growth year on year	%	32	29.1	33.9	34.9	31.1	24.7	17.8	−8.2	33.0
Imports	US$bn	0.8	1.05	1.39	1.68	1.81	2.1	2.09	2.34	2.55
Growth year on year	%	13.2	31.3	32.4	20.9	7.7	16.0	−0.5	12.0	9.0
Contracted FDI	US$bn	0.12	0.29	0.51	0.89	1.05	1.05	0.46	N/A	N/A
Growth year on year	%	71.4	141.7	75.9	74.5	18.0	0.0	−56.2	N/A	N/A
Used FDI	US$bn	0.08	0.12	0.21	0.36	0.46	0.62	0.26	0.23	0.18
Growth year on year	%	45.6	50.0	75.0	71.4	27.8	34.8	−58.1	−11.5	−21.7
New FIEs	No	124	174	157	224	223	141	69	21	25
Growth year on year	%	65.3	40.3	−9.8	42.7	−0.4	−36.8	−51.1	−69.6	19.0

Sources National Bureau of Statistics China Statistical Yearbooks, city government publications, media sources deemed reliable. *N/A* is data not announced in the city government's annual economic and social report and growth data is calculated based on in house data for the previous year. May be available from other sources

ANHUI PROVINCE
安徽省

Hu Jintao, China's president (2011), is a native of Anhui, as is Wu Bangguo, chairman of the Standing Committee of the National People's Congress (2011).

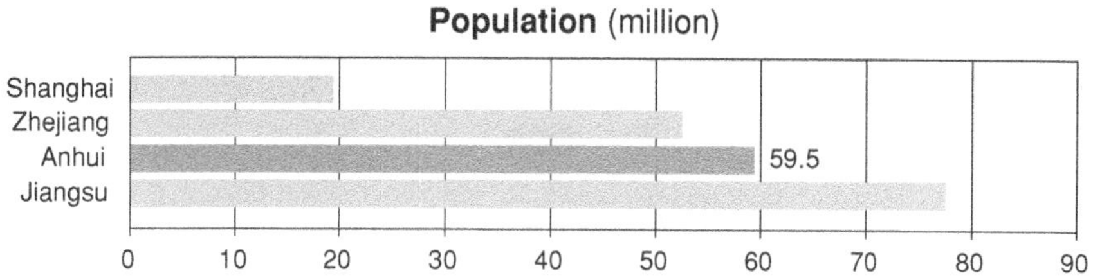

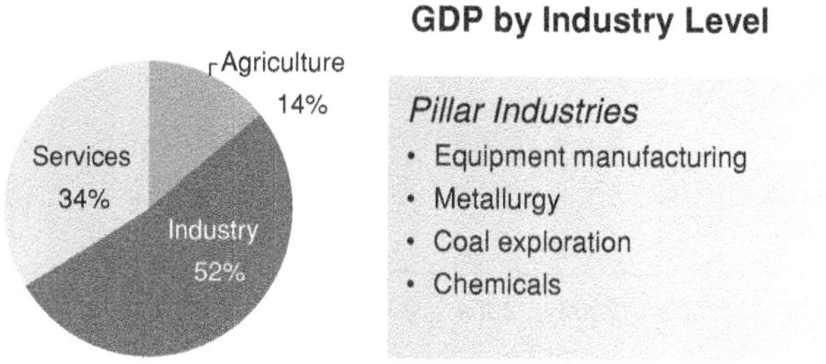

Although most economists set a 3-h drive from Shanghai as the range of the YRD's economic radius, Anhui province, out to the west, is looking to join the regional collective. With close proximity to Shanghai, Anhui has long been a source of migrant labor for the city. The economy is still mostly agricultural, but the province is also a national base for the material industry and a large provider of coal and energy to eastern China. Anhui boasts vast raw material resources, including iron, copper, and limestone reserves that rank among the top five largest in China. With its strong resource base, close proximity to Shanghai and Jiangsu and Zhejiang provinces, Anhui's future development prospects are looking bright.

While the province's capital is Hefei, one of China's four main "science and education bases," business is spread throughout the industrial regions close to the Yangtze River—including the cities of Anqing (the provincial capital until 1946), Huainan, Bengbu, Ma'anshan and Wuhu. For example, the headquarters of the province's most famous corporation, Chery Automotive, is in Wuhu.

2.27 Economy

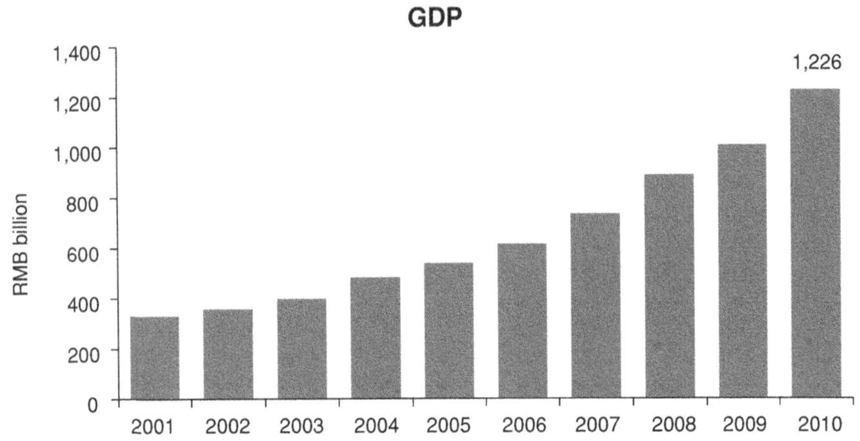

Anhui's economy has been growing rapidly in recent years, with 22% growth year-on-year in 2010 to reach RMB 1.23 trillion. Anhui is a major exporter both within China and internationally. Total exports increased 39.7% year-on-year in 2010, approximately 30% were processed exports (raw materials were imported, processed into ready-made parts and exported).

2.27.1 *Anhui's Exports by Continent*

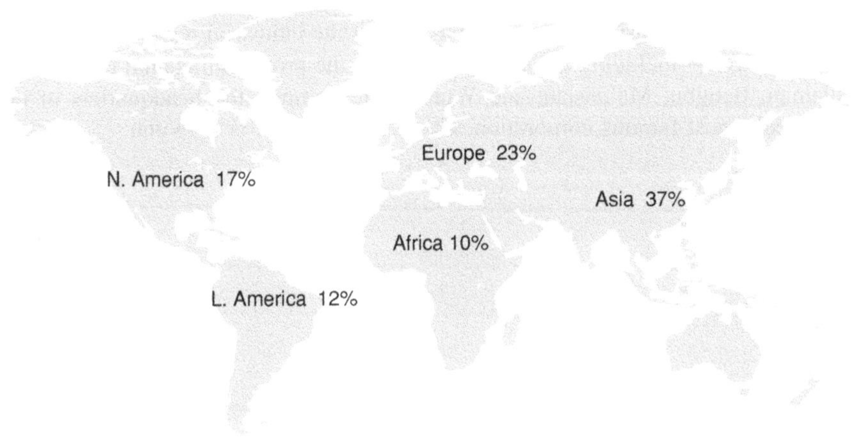

Foreign investment amounted to approximately US $20 billion during the 11th Five-Year Plan (2005–2010), according to the Anhui Development and Reform Commission. While Anhui's foreign investment levels remains the lowest in the YRD, it has been increasingly rapidly in recent years.

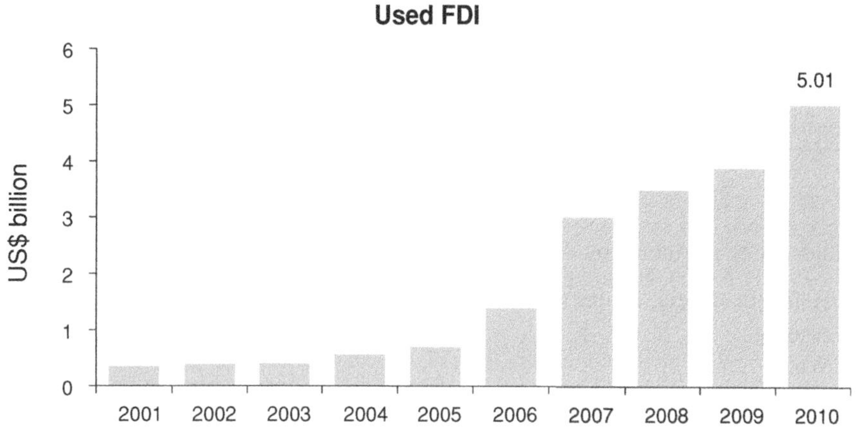

2.28 Infrastructure

Anhui's airports by passenger throughput (2010)

City	Airport	Passenger throughput (# people)	Change y-on-y (%)
Hefei	Luogang	3,817,051	19.1
Huangshan	Tunxi	343,033	20.3
Fuyang	Fuyang	108,630	524.1
Anqing	Anqing	76,330	152.9

Source National Airport Throughput Rankings Civil Aviation Administration of China, March 2011

Selected industrial products made in Anhui (2010)

Product	Amount produced		Growth Y-on-Y (%)
Rubber tire	37.44	Million units	116
Fabric	1.09	Billion meters	68
Air conditioner	16.67	Million units	63
Car	12.45	Million units	36
Metal cutting machine tools	0.03	Million units	33
Fridge	20.79	Million units	32
Power cable	1,282.80	Million meters	31

(continued)

(continued)

Product	Amount produced		Growth Y-on-Y (%)
Washing machine	12.67	Million units	29
Sulfuric acid	4.40	Million tons	25
10 non-ferrous metals	1.69	Million tons	21
Chemical fiber	22.00	1,000 tons	19
Synthetic detergent	7.46	Million tons	17
Yarn	56.50	1,000 tons	15
Steel	24.46	Million tons	14
Cement	78.74	Million tons	13

Major cities in Anhui (by GDP) include:

- Hefei (Provincial capital)
- Anqing
- Wuhu
- Ma'anshan

2.28.1 Resources

Anhui Provincial Government
apps.ah.gov.cn

Anhui Development and Reform Commission
www.ahpc.gov.cn

Anhui Provincial Foreign Trade and Economic Cooperation Bureau
www.ahbofcom.gov.cn

Historical Context

The province of Anhui was formed in the seventeenth century and before that, there was no coherent concept of "Anhui." Northern Anhui was firmly a part of the North China Plain in terms of culture, while southern Anhui was closer to Hubei and southern Jiangsu province in culture. The hills of southeastern Anhui have a unique and distinct cultural sphere all on its own. Central Anhui constituted most of the fertile and densely-populated Huai River watershed.

Present day Anhui was first settled by the Han people and this was their first contact with southern China. After the fall of the Han dynasty in 220, unrest led the Han people to continue to migrate. The fourth century also saw an influx of nomadic tribes from Central Asia into north China which began several centuries of political division for northern and southern China. Being at the juncture of north and south, what comprises modern Anhui changed hands frequently and was politically bisected by the various tribes.

The Manchu Qing Dynasty conquered China in 1644 and established Jiangnan province, which eventually was divided in 1666 to form Jiangsu and Anhui provinces. This was the beginning of the modern Anhui, which over the years has maintained almost the same borders.

In the early 1850s, the Yellow River made one of its great changes in course, flowing north into the Bohai Sea instead of south into the Yellow Sea. This created a loss of water for the Huai Basin in Northern Anhui and resulted in many uprisings by the local farmers. This unrest, together with the Taiping Rebellion, resulted in widespread devastation for Anhui province. In 1938, the Yellow River was temporarily diverted south, purposefully this time, by the Nationalist government in the hopes of holding off the advancing Japanese. But the river waters continued south to the Hongze Lake on the Anhui border, flooding an enormous area and claiming 900,000 lives.

Anhui's provincial administration experienced relatively greater leadership turnover than other provinces in the 1950s and 1960s. During the Cultural Revolution, Anhui supported many of the radical programs of the time, but by the late 1970s, had become a base for many of the moderate reforms advocated by the post-Mao leadership.

Anhui by numbers

	Unit	2001	2002	2003	2004	2005	2006	2007	2008	2009	2010
Population	m people	63.28	63.38	64.1	64.61	65.16	65.94	66.78	61.4	61.3	59.5
GDP	RMBbn	329.01	356.9	397.3	481.3	537.58	614.19	734.57	887.42	1,005.29	1,226.34
Proportion : primary industry	%	22.9	21.7	18.9	19.4	17.9	16.7	16.5	16	14.9	14.1
: secondary industry	%	43	43.5	44.8	45.1	41.6	43.3	44.7	46.6	48.8	52.1
: tertiary industry	%	34.1	34.8	36.3	35.5	40.5	40	38.8	37.4	36.3	33.8
GDP growth year on year	%	8.6	8.48	11.32	21.14	11.69	14.25	19.6	20.81	13.28	21.99
Per capita GDP (all residents)	RMB	5,221	5,623	6,457	7,768	8,597	10,044	12,015	14,485	16,391	15,788
Fixed asset investment	RMBbn	96.26	113.33	147.76	191.42	252.1	354.47	510.59	678.89	926.32	1,184.94
Growth year on year	%	11	17.73	30.38	29.55	31.7	40.61	44.04	32.96	36.45	27.92
Industrial production value	RMBbn	119.15	129.05	144.56	173.6	183.32	220.05	275.21	N/A	N/A	N/A
Growth year on year	%	9.9	10.3	12.2	12.5	20.4	19.1	21.7	N/A	N/A	N/A
Per capita disposable income of urban residents	RMB	5,669	6,032	6,778	7,511	8,471	9,771	11,474	12,990	14,085	15,788
Growth year on year	%	7.1	6.4	12.37	10.81	12.78	15.35	17.43	13.21	8.43	12.09
Retail sales	RMBbn	114.3	122.88	133.1	150.3	176.5	202.94	240.37	296.55	352.78	415.15
Growth year on year	%	8.4	7.51	8.32	12.92	17.43	14.98	18.44	23.37	18.96	17.68
Exports	US$bn	2.28	2.45	3.06	3.94	5.19	6.84	8.82	11.35	8.89	12.42
Growth year on year	%	5.1	7.5	24.9	28.76	31.73	31.79	28.95	28.68	−21.67	39.71
Imports	US$bn	1.34	1.73	2.88	3.27	3.93	5.41	7.11	9.08	6.78	11.86
Growth year on year	%	13.9	29.1	66.47	13.54	20.18	37.66	31.42	27.71	−25.33	74.93
Contracted FDI	US$bn	N/A	N/A	N/A	1.21	1.55	2.5	3.57	2.1	2.09	2.16
Growth year on year	%	N/A	N/A	N/A	17.9	29	60.9	42.8	-33.2	1.6	50.1
Used FDI	US$bn	0.34	0.38	0.39	0.55	0.69	1.39	3	3.49	3.88	5.01
Growth year on year	%	5.7	11.76	2.63	41.03	25.45	101.45	115.83	16.33	11.17	29.12
New FIEs	No	260	338	431	472	421	592	520	256	303	281
Growth year on year	%	5.3	30	27.51	9.51	−10.81	40.62	−12.16	−50.77	18.36	−7.26

Sources National Bureau of Statistics China Statistical Yearbooks, city government publications, media sources deemed reliable. *N/A* is data not announced in the city government's annual economic and social report and growth data is calculated based on in house data for the previous year. May be available from other sources

Hefei 合肥

Anhui's Coastal City

Hefei was identified as the number one fastest growing city in China at the Economist summit in November 2010

Hefei, the capital city of Anhui Province, is considered one of the four main "science and education bases" in China—along with Beijing, Chengdu and Xi'an. The city's proportion of total provincial GDP jumped from 17.3 to 22% between 2006 and 2010 and the city aims to account for 25% of provincial GDP by 2015.

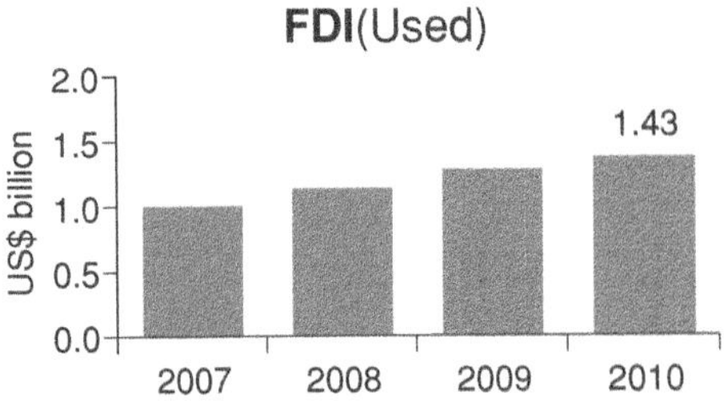

Used FDI was US$1.43 billion in 2010, with 72 new foreign-invested enterprises. These numbers, while growing fast, pale in comparison to nearby cities.

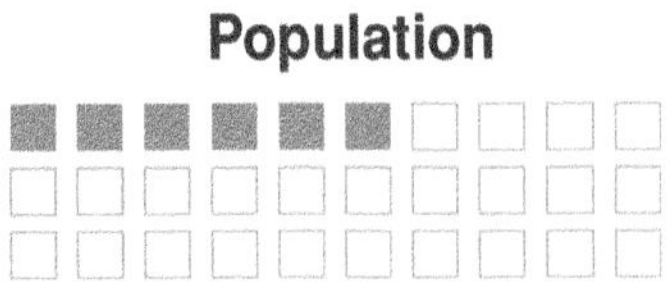

5.70 million

2.29 Infrastructure

2.29.1 Railways

Hefei is connected with the Hefei–Wuhan high- speed railway, Hefei–Nanjing high-speed railway, Huainan railroad, Hefei–Jiujiang railroad, and Nanjing–Xi'an railroad. With the Shanghai–Wuhan–Chengdu high-speed train, travel time from Hefei to Shanghai is about 2.5 h. The Hefei–Bengbu section of the Beijing–Shanghai express railway is expected to star t running before February 2012 and travel time from Hefei to Beijing will be reduced to 5 h.

2.29.2 Ports and Waterways

The Hefei Port is one of the 28 main river ports in China, and one of the nine major river ports in Anhui. It is located in Central Anhui between the Yangtze River and Huaihe River. Shipping ocean containers from Hefei is a less expensive option than shipment from Wuhu, Shanghai or Beijing. Currently there are four port operation zones at the Hefei Port.

2.30 Economy and Investment

Hefei's popularity for FDI is expanding fast. The average scale of FDIs increased significantly in 2011—while 2010 saw 18 projects valued at US $200 million, mid-2011 saw 9 projects valued at twice that amount (US $492.81 million).

The eight key industries in Hefei are: auto-making, equipment manufacturing, household appliance, chemicals, IT and software, new materials, biotechnology and new medicine, and finally food and processing of agricultural/sideline products. Of these, household appliance production is the leading industry and the city aims to be the "world's leading home appliances manufacturing base." New energy vehicles are receiving a major push from the government, with goals including production capacity for 500,000 new energy vehicles by 2015.

Selected 2015 industrial output goals by industry (12th Five-Year Plan)

Electronic information	RMB 250 billion
New energy	RMB 200 billion
Home appliances	RMB 200 billion
Vehicle and auto parts	RMB 150 billion
Equipment manufacturing	RMB 150 billion

Hefei High-tech Industrial Development Zone (Hefei HIDZ), located southeast of Hefei, has received a good deal of attention in recent years. The zone was opened to member nations of the Asia Pacific Economic Cooperation in 2007 and has a software park, university hi-tech park, biomedical park, automobile park and an incubator park.

Hefei will have the second fastest population growth in China between 2009 and 2014 (46% between start and end year), according to Economist Intelligence Unit predictions in November 2010, a boom that will fuel city GDP growth and present social challenges. Industrial pollution in Hefei is also a challenge for the city—it currently ranks seventh highest in the nation, above cities like Wuhan, according to the same source.

2.30.1 Spotlight: One of China's Four Science and Education Bases

Hefei is considered one of the four main "science and education bases" in China—along with Beijing, Chengdu and Xi'an. The city has three national laboratories, second in number only to Beijing. The National Laboratory for Nuclear Fusion is administered by the Hefei Institute of Physical Sciences, Institute of Plasma Physics, while the National Synchrotron Radiation Laboratory and the Hefei National Laboratory for Physical Sciences at the Microscale are administered by the University of Science and Technology of China. In addition, Hefei is part of the first group of technical innovation experimental cities and the Ministry of Science and Technology and the Chinese Academy of Sciences are in the process of creating a 50 km^2 "science city of China" by 2020.

2.30.2 Resources

Hefei Government
http://www.hefei.gov.cn

Hefei National Laboratory for Physical Sciences at the Microscale
http://en.hfnl.ustc.edu.cn/

Key Industries

- Autos and autoparts
- Equipment manufacturing
- Household appliance
- Chemicals
- IT and software
- New materials
- Biotechnology and new medicine
- Food and processing of agricultural/sideline products

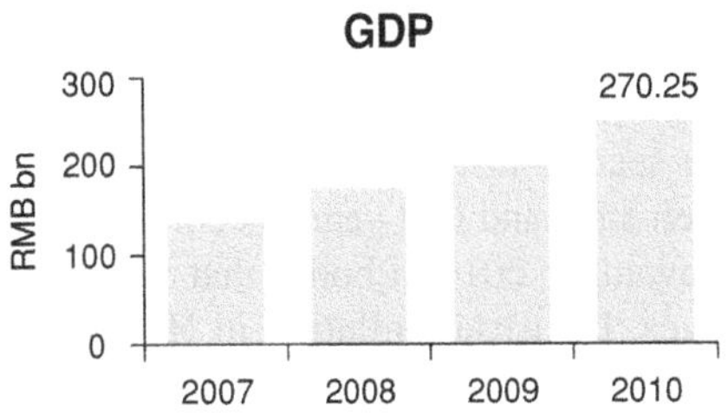

Hefei's GDP was RMB270.25 billion in 2010, a 28.56 percent increase year-on-year.

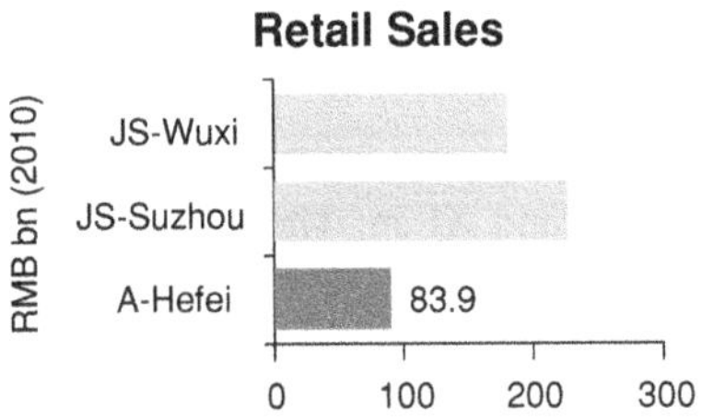

Hefei's retail sales reached RMB83.9 billion in 2010, significant growth year-on-year.

Hefei by numbers

Item	Unit	2002	2003	2004	2005	2006	2007	2008	2009	2010
Population	m people	4.48	4.57	4.45	4.56	4.70	4.79	5.01	5.10	5.70
GDP	RMBbn	41.24	47.78	58.97	85.36	107.39	133.42	166.65	210.21	270.25
Proportion: primary industry	%	9.70	8.50	9.20	6.20	5.80	6.00	6.30	5.20	4.90
: secondary industry	%	50.10	49.90	50.40	44.80	47.50	48.80	50.20	52.60	53.90
: tertiary industry	%	40.20	41.60	40.40	49.00	46.70	45.20	43.50	42.20	41.20
GDP growth year on year	%	13.10	13.30	16.20	16.90	17.50	18.10	17.20	26.14	28.56
Per capita GDP (all residents)	RMB	9,203	10,464	13,261	18,732	22,854	27,854	33,263	41,218	47,412
Fixed asset investment	RMBbn	16.87	25.51	36.15	49.53	82.48	131.04	183.86	246.84	306.70
Growth year on year	%	19.30	51.24	41.71	37.01	66.53	58.87	40.31	34.25	24.25
Industrial production value	RMBbn	17.56	18.48	22.94	29.22	109.85	148.84	208.00	274.92	376.89
Growth year on year	%	14.70	13.30	16.80	17.20	22.50	35.49	39.75	32.17	37.09
Per capita disposable income of urban residents	RMB	7,145	7,785	8,610	9,684	11,013	13,427	15,591	17,158	19,051
Growth year on year	%	10.30	8.96	10.60	12.47	13.72	21.92	16.12	10.05	11.03
Retail sales	RMBbn	18.48	20.74	23.98	32.44	38.43	46.90	58.84	70.34	83.90
Growth year on year	%	12.30	12.23	15.62	35.28	18.46	22.04	25.45	19.55	19.28
Exports	US$bn	1.50	1.82	2.19	2.79	3.41	4.30	5.43	4.45	5.63
Growth year on year	%	6.50	21.33	20.33	27.40	22.22	26.10	26.28	−18.08	26.48
Imports	US$bn	0.80	1.20	1.32	1.39	1.47	1.95	2.28	1.98	4.33
Growth year on year	%	23.70	50.00	10.00	5.30	5.76	32.65	16.82	−13.08	118.79
Contracted FDI	US$bn	0.23	0.25	0.27	0.35	0.92	1.15	0.78	N/A	7.43
Growth year on year	%	4.50	8.70	8.00	29.63	162.86	25.00	−32.52	N/A	103.00
Used FDI	US$bn	0.18	0.26	0.32	0.41	0.72	1.01	1.20	1.30	1.43
Growth year on year	%	58.80	44.44	23.08	28.13	75.61	40.28	18.81	8.33	10.00
New FIEs	No	73.00	102.00	101.00	91.00	155.00	122.00	70.00	59.00	72.00
Growth year on year	%	23.70	39.73	-0.98	-9.90	70.33	−21.29	−42.62	−15.71	22.03

Sources National Bureau of Statistics China Statistical Yearbooks, city government publications, media sources deemed reliable. *N/A* is data not announced in the city government's annual economic and social report and growth data is calculated based on in house data for the previous year. May be available from other sources

Chapter 3
Establishing Business

What are the investment structures available?

- Representative offices
- Joint ventures
- Wholly foreign-owned enterprises
- Foreign-invested commercial enterprises

Dezan Shira & Associates et al. (eds.), *The Yangtze River Delta*, China Briefing,
DOI: 10.1007/978-3-642-27624-8_3, © Asia Briefing Ltd. 2012

Setting up a company in China is a complex and bureaucratic process, much more so than in the EU or North America, so seek professional advice. Here, we overview the investment structures available and the pros and cons of each.

3.1 The Foreign Investment Catalogue

The Chinese government both encourages and discourages a variety of investments, according to the demands and the needs of the country at that particular time. These sectors are detailed in the Foreign Investment Catalogue, the most recent version of which is 2007.[1] In April 2011, a new draft guideline for foreign investment was released by the Legislative Affairs Office of the State Council, but at time of print has not yet been approved.

Each of the categories broadly include the following:

3.1.1 Encouraged Foreign Investments

- Logistics and service outsourcing
- Banking and investment, finance and accounting and IT consulting services on the international economy, science and technology and environmental protection
- Projects for new and high technology, advanced and applicable technology which can improve performance of products and increase the techno-economic efficiency of enterprises, or produce new equipment and new material where the domestic capacity is deficient.
- Projects related to new agricultural technology, construction of energy sources, transport and raw materials for industry
- Projects that involve integrated use of China's resources or use of renewable resources, involving new technology or equipment for preventing and controlling environmental pollution
- Projects that meet market demands, can promote the quality of products, enter into new markets, or help products to compete in international markets
- Projects that increase development of construction and management of urban public facilities, sewage and waste treatment

[1] The catalogue is available at: http://www.fdi.gov.cn/pub/FDI_EN/Laws/GeneralLawsandRegulations/MinisterialRulings/P020071121358108121219.pdf

3.1.2 *Restricted Foreign Investments*

- Projects that can have an adverse effect on energy conservation or on the environment
- Mineral extraction projects, projects already developed in China, where the technology has already been imported and where capacity can meet market demand

3.1.3 *Prohibited Foreign Investments*

- Duplication, manufacture, or processing of Chinese treasured goods, such as rare plant breeds and traditionally crafted teas
- Power generating projects
- Futures companies

3.2 Set Up Considerations

When contemplating setting up a business in China, one needs to consider what structure to use. But before doing so, you must first consider why you want to make an investment in China. Some common motivations include customer pull and operational efficiencies. After thoroughly laying out your motivations and goals, you can then determine your strategy and decide on the structure that best meets your objectives.

When choosing an appropriate investment vehicle, many factors must be considered, as these will lead to different legal and tax considerations. You will need to address questions such as:

- Do you need to invoice locally for services or products?
- Are you getting a feel for the market or have you decided to commit to a larger scale operation?
- Are you planning to set up a production oriented entity or do you need only a representation in the country to carry out market research or liaison activities?
- Will you be involved in trading, manufacturing, services or a combination of these?
- Is the sector you are investing in fully opened to foreign participation or do you still require a local partner?

- Would you need to conduct the business alone, or would you require a Chinese company chipping in with assets or distribution networks?
- Where should you be? You will need to consider issues such as proximity to Chinese suppliers and raw materials, customers, ports and related infrastructure, as well as cost-related concerns or available incentives.

Once you've clearly defined the needs and goals of your China investment, it's time to consider the legal form your China entity should take. Foreign investors have several choices for structuring a China enterprise: the representative office, the joint venture, the wholly foreign-owned enterprise and the foreign-invested commercial enterprise. These structures have different features that can help or hinder your China venture, so choosing the appropriate vehicle from the outset will be invaluable for the long-term success of any investment. The procedures for setting up a presence in China are quite complex and you should not contemplate doing it without expert advice. Most companies engage the services of one of the major international consulting firms based in China or one of the larger local firms.

3.2.1 Representative Offices

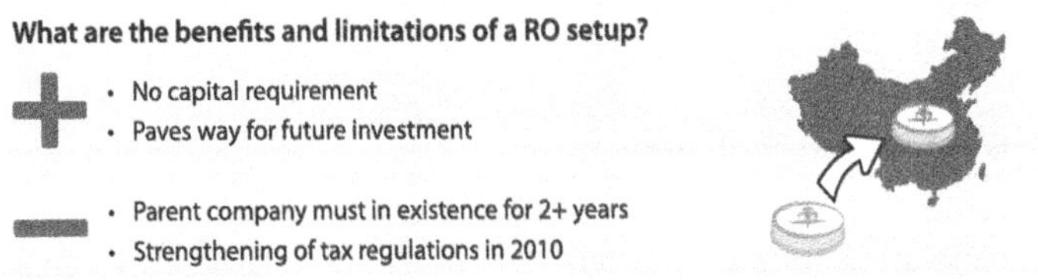

The representative office (RO) is the least dynamic of the entities for establishing a foreign presence in China. The administrative regulations on ROs (Administrative Regulations), issued by the State Council in November 2010 and taking effect in March 2011, specify that the activities that ROs are permitted to engage in include (i) market research, display and publicity activities that relate to company product or services; and (ii) contact activities that relate to company product sales or service provision and domestic procurement and investment.

ROs are forbidden from engaging in any profit-seeking activities except for those which China has agreed on in international agreements or treaties. As such, an RO may not directly invoice for sales or services in China and can only interact with Chinese businesses indirectly.

While ROs have little control over the movement and sale of goods and services, as the extended arm of overseas parent companies, some benefits and advantages of having a representative office include the fact that they have no registered capital requirement and can be very helpful in facilitating market entry by coordinating sourcing activities and marketing and establishing trade ties between your parent company overseas and your entities based in China. ROs can also act as a liaison in matters relating to orders, shipping payments of taxes, repatriation of money and so on. In a less tangible way, they can offer a sense of the domestic market and help determine whether China's 1.3 billion people and its complex business and legal structure are profitably navigable for your company.

From January 1, 2010, ROs are no longer exempt from corporate income tax in China. A circular issued by the State Administration of Taxation on February 20, 2010 explicitly stipulates that ROs must pay corporate income tax on their taxable income, as well as sales tax and VAT.

3.2.2 *Joint Ventures*

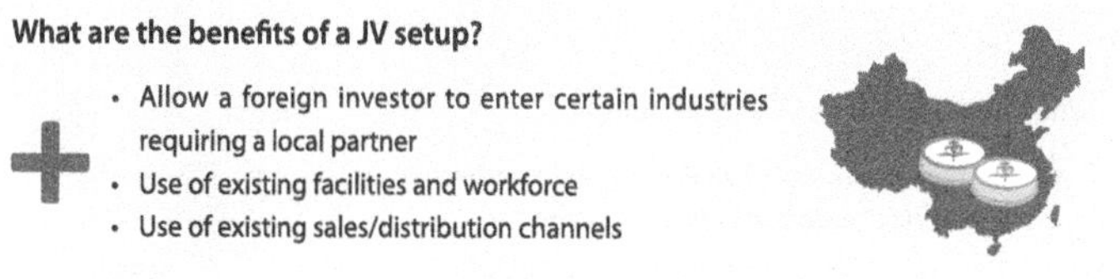

Forming a joint venture (JV) in China can be a successful endeavor as long as each side's goals, contributions and responsibilities are mutual and understood. It's crucial for foreign investors to understand the purposes of joint ventures and whether their Chinese partner is capable of fulfilling them. The popular Chinese idiom "same bed, different dreams" has become the failed joint venture's mantra.

3.2.2.1 Types of JVs

There are two types of JVs in China: the equity JV and the cooperative JV, sometimes known as the contractual JV.

An EJV is a joint venture between Chinese and foreign partners where the profits and losses are distributed between the parties in proportion to their respective equity interests in the EJV. The foreign partner should hold at least 25% of the equity interest in the registered capital of the EJV. The company enjoys limited liability as a "Chinese legal person."

The CJV is a very flexible FIE where Chinese and foreign investors have more contractual freedom to structure cooperation. It is a joint venture between Chinese and foreign investors where the profits and losses are distributed between the parties in accordance with the specific provisions in the CJV contract, not necessarily in proportion to their respective equity interests in the CJV. CJVs have the option to operate either as a limited liability company or as a non-legal person.

There are significant operational differences between the contracts and laws governing EJVs and CJVs, including in terms of liability status, management structure, contractual obligations, capital contributions, profit sharing and equity ratios and reclaiming capital investment.

3.2.3 Wholly Foreign-Owned Enterprises

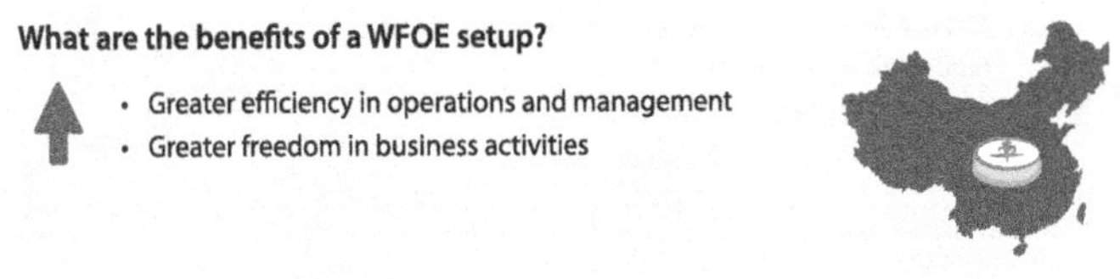

The wholly foreign-owned enterprise (WFOE) has become the investment vehicle of choice for the international investor wanting to engage in the manufacturing, service or trade sectors in China. In addition to the WFOE's expansive business scope, its unrivaled popularity arises from multiple other factors:

- 100% foreign ownership and control
- Security of technology and intellectual property rights
- Self-developed internal structure
- Insertion of existing company culture
- Profit repatriation
- Domestic sales

3.2.4 Foreign-Invested Commercial Enterprises

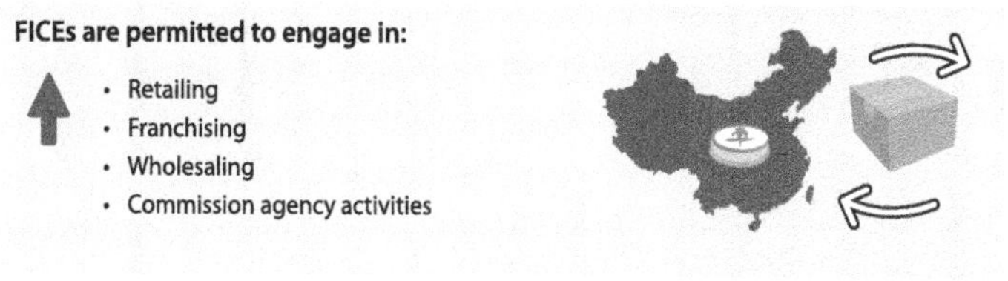

To engage in import and export as well as domestic distribution (i.e. retail, wholesale and franchising trade activities) in China, foreign investors can establish a foreign-invested commercial enterprise (FICE).

A FICE can be a WFOE or a JV. A WFOE or JV can be established to engage exclusively in commercial activities, or combine FICE activities with other business activities, such as manufacturing and providing services.

Generally, a FICE is inexpensive to establish and can be of great assistance to the foreign investor in combining both sourcing and quality control activities with a purchasing and export facility, thus providing much more control and reaction times than if sourcing purely while based overseas.

FICEs that engage in the retail business can, upon permission, engage in the retail of goods, import of goods dealt in by the FICE itself, purchase of domestic products for export, and other relevant ancillary business, but are prohibited from dealing in tobacco.

FICEs that engage in the wholesale business can engage in the wholesale of goods, commission agency (except auctioning), import and export of goods, and other relevant ancillary business, but are prohibited from dealing in salt and tobacco.

Limitations apply to FICEs dealing in specific products such as books, periodicals, newspapers, pharmaceutical products, agricultural chemicals, agricultural films, chemical fertilizers, processed oil, grains, vegetable oil, edible sugar and cotton. If a foreign investor has more than 30 retail stores in China and distributes products mentioned above from different brands or suppliers, the foreign investor's share in a retail enterprise is limited to 49%.

References

For more detailed information, please see Asia Briefing's Technical Guide series at www.asiabriefing.com.

Choosing Your China structure

Type of structure	Abbrev.	Legal status	Common purpose(s)	Pros	Cons
Representative office	RO	No legal personality	Market research, planning longer-term ventures, liaison with home country companies	Inexpensive to set up	Cannot invoice locally in RMB
				Allows exploration of the market and liaison activity	Must recruit staff from local agency
Wholly foreign owned enterprise	WFOE	Limited liability legal personality	Most manufacturing businesses (for China sales or export), some service businesses	100% ownership and control	Need to fund registered capital requirement
				More flexible business scope	
					Development of China sales operations on your own
				Security of technology/IP	
				Development of own infrastructure	
				Insertion of existing company culture	
				Allowed to convert RMB into foreign currency for profit repatriation	
Foreign invested commercial enterprise	FICE	Limited liability legal personality	WFOE or JV mainly used for trading, distribution, and retail	As for normal WFOE or JV	As for normal WFOE or JV
				Specialised structure for trading, retailing and distribution	
Joint venture	JV	Limited liability legal personality (in most cases)	When restrictions require local partner, or when they can offer e.g. sales and distributions channels	Use of existing facilities and workforce	Management can be awkward
				Use of existing sales/distribution channels	Inheriting staff liabilities
				Eager to secure long-term export sales	Over inflation of assets or sales in planning
					Technology transfer/IP/ management risks
					Split profits

What are the main business taxes in China?

- Corporate Income Tax
- Withholding Tax
- Value-added Tax
- Business Tax
- Consumption Tax

The People's Republic of China levies a wide range of taxes including income taxes (corporate income tax and withholding tax) and turnover taxes (value-added tax, business tax and consumption tax). Here, we provide an overview of these taxes.

3.3 Corporate Income Tax

Corporate income tax is calculated against the net income in a financial year after deducting reasonable business costs and losses—in other words it is effectively a tax on profits. It is settled on an annual basis but is often paid quarterly with adjustments either refunded or carried forward to the next year. The final calculation is based on the year-end audit.

The income tax rate for all companies in China, both foreign and domestic, is 25%.

3.3.1 Tax Incentives

Some tax incentives are listed below:

- "Encouraged" high-tech enterprises are eligible for a reduced CIT rate of 15%
- Small and low-profit enterprises enjoy a reduced CIT rate of 20%
- Research and development expenses can be deducted from the taxable income by as much as 150% of the total amount
- 200% deduction apples to salary paid to disabled employee
- 200% CIT deductions applies to the wages paid to disabled employees

Reduced CIT rates

Circumstance	Reduced CIT rate (%)
"Encouraged" high-tech enterprises	15
Small and low-profit enterprises	20

Tax income deductions

Circumstance	Tax income deduction rate (%)
Salary paid to disabled employees	200
R&D expenses	150

3.4 Withholding Tax

Withholding tax is a PRC tax levied on passive income (i.e. dividends, bonuses, other equity investment gains, interests, rentals, royalties, transfer of property) received by non-resident enterprises from China.

Pay close attention to the difference between resident and non-resident enterprises.

A non-resident enterprise is an enterprise that is set up in accordance with the laws of a foreign country and whose place of effective management is not located in China, and:

- has an office or business premises in China and receives incomes that have no actual connection to its China-based office or business premises (e.g. a foreign enterprise has an office in Beijing, but its taxable business activities were conducted in Guangzhou independent of the Beijing office); or
- does not have an office or business premises in China, but derives incomes sourced from China.

The withholding income tax rate for non-tax resident enterprises in China is 20% under the Corporate Income Tax Law. This was reduced to 10% under the detailed implementation regulations of the CIT law. For countries that have signed tax treaties with China, such as Hong Kong, rates differ.

The China enterprise remitting the fund overseas should be the withholding agent for the withholding tax. If the withholding agent fails to fulfill its obligation to withhold tax, the non-resident enterprise is required to file and pay CIT to local tax authorities.

3.5 Value-Added Tax

All enterprises and individuals engaged in the sale of goods, provision of processing, repairs and replacement services, and import of goods in China shall pay VAT. There are a few exemptions, such as self-produced agricultural products sold by agricultural producers, contraceptive medicines and devices, and antique books. However, pretty much every business will be liable for this tax.

VAT taxpayers are divided into general taxpayers and small-scale taxpayers. Taxpayers with an annual sales value exceeding the annual sales threshold for small-scale taxpayers set by MOF and SAT must apply to the tax department for recognition as general taxpayers.

The annual sales threshold for small scale taxpayers is:

RMB 500,000 (for enterprises engaged primarily in the production o f goods or the provision of taxable services)
RMB 800,000 (for enterprises engaged in the wholesaling or retailing of goods)

3.5.1 VAT Calculation for General Taxpayers

The VAT rate for general taxpayers is generally 17, or 13% for some goods. VAT payable relies on two figures: output VAT and input VAT. Output VAT is that payable on the services and goods sold by a company. Input VAT is that payable on the goods and services a company buys from another supplier.

The input VAT is used as a credit against the output tax levied on selling the goods. The VAT payable shall be the output VAT for the period, after deducting the input VAT for the period, i.e.:

VAT payable = output VAT − input VAT

VAT calculation for small scale taxpayers

The current VAT rate for small scale taxpayers is 3%. As such taxpayers cannot deduct input VAT, the formula is as follows:

VAT payable = sales value × tax rate (i.e. 3%)

3.6 Business Tax

This is a tax payable against turnover by all enterprises and individuals undertaking the following business: providing taxable services, including communications, transport, construction, finance and insurance, telecoms, culture, entertainment and service industries; transferring intangible assets; and selling real estate.

Businesses must be careful if they are selling goods and services simultaneously, as in these cases there are complicated criteria to judge whether business tax or VAT is applicable.

Only a very few items are excluded from turnover. Rates of business tax vary from 3 to 20%, dependent on industry.

Business tax applies to services performed where either the service provider or the service recipient is located in China, without regard to where the service is actually being rendered. Business tax is usually calculated, filed and paid to the local tax bureau every month. When first registering for business tax, the tax bureau will issue a form showing all the taxes applicable.

3.7 Consumption Tax

Consumption tax applies whenever certain luxury or other goods are manufactured, processed or imported. Unlike VAT, which is levied across various stages of the value-addition chain, consumption tax is levied only once, with consumers ultimately carrying the burden of the tax. Tax rates vary considerably with the product, for example, cigars are imposed a 36% rate, and motor vehicle tires 3%. The tax paid is computed directly as a cost and cannot be refunded (except in rare cases upon the receipt of a consumption tax special invoice from the domestic supplier for consumption taxes paid for export goods).

Be careful if you are processing taxable goods for others, since you are liable to withhold and pay consumption tax based on the value of the raw material and your processing fee. Consumption tax should be filed and paid monthly.

References

For more detailed information, please see Asia Briefing's Technical Guide series at www.asiabriefingmedia.com.

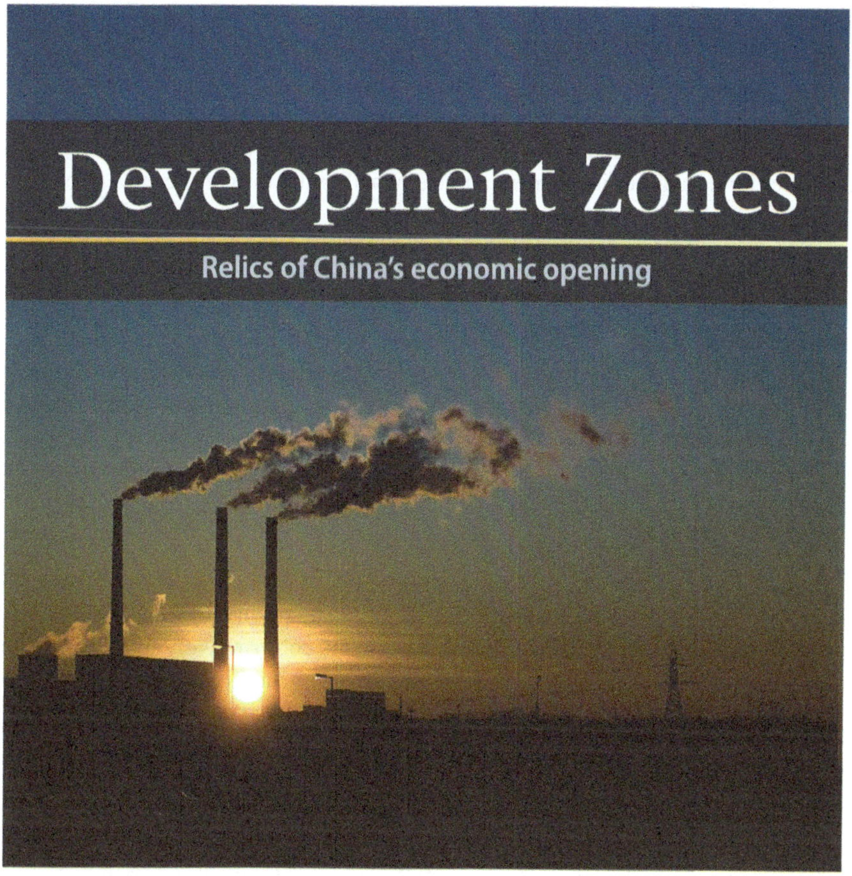

Why invest in a Development Zone?

- Preferential policies
- Support & participation of government
- Autonomy
- Resource availability
- Hubs of technology, learning and innovation

China's first development zones were established in the 1970s and few can deny the significance these economic areas have had in building the global powerhouse China is today. The origin of development zones in China can be traced back to 1978, when the country's leaders were searching fora path to wealth and development to lift the country from economic and social disparity.

Development zones are not a Chinese creation, but China in particular has found tremendous success with this economic tool. Historically, the liberal business environment in these areas allowed foreign businesses to operate more comfortably in the Chinese business environment, sheltered from the bureaucracy and red tape that often characterizes the rest of the country. Development zones are successful in China primarily because of the central Chinese government's strong support and the relative autonomy of zone managers.

The first development zones, hand-selected along the country's southern coast in Shenzhen, Zhuhai, Shantou and Xiamen, acted as doorways for the government to attract foreign direct investment and test whether the formerly centrally-planned economy could transition to a more liberal and capitalist model. These zones focused on aiding in manufacture for export to bolster the local economy without posing too significant a threat to state-owned enterprises.

The original drivers of the success of development zones are perhaps less relevant today than they were 30 years ago. Foreign investment in China pours into all regions of the country, not just development zones. As well, the 2008 Tax Reform took a hit at the tax incentives offered in development zones. Finally, foreign companies are increasingly interested in domestic sales, not solely focused on the exporting for which development zones were originally designed.

The original drivers of the success of development zones are perhaps less relevant today than they were 30 years ago.

Regardless, the convenience of established infrastructure, reserved land and one-stop services available in development zones streamlines entry into China. For a manufacturer, an investment outside of a zone is comparatively more expensive and complicated, considering logistical and governmental issues.

3.8 Types of Development Zones

The largest and most comprehensive types of development zones are Special Economic Zones (SEZs) and Economic and Technological Development Zones (ETDZs).

3.9 Classifications of Development Zones

Development zones are often classified by industry (high-tech, heavy, light, agriculture or service) or by region (YRD, Bohai Ring, Central, etc.), but the most defined of all classification systems is administrative level.

The central, provincial and regional governments play important roles in the establishment of development zones, with local governments often appointing state-owned enterprises (SOEs) to run these areas. The central government influences tax advantages as well as accreditation of zones. In order to be certified a national zone, the area needs to meet certain requirements—exact performance measures and related targets are not published but parks are most likely assessed based on:

Types of development zones

Development zone type	Description	Example
Special Economic Zones (SEZ)	Large designated managed areas which benefit from special economic regulations, like tax incentives, and also generally offer duty-free benefits	Shenzhen SEZ • China's very first SEZ • Fifth highest GDP amongst all of China's administrative regions
Economic and Technological Development Zones (ETDZ)	ETDZs are similar to SEZs but are generally smaller in region and focused in specific industries or sectors	Lianyungang ETDZ • Location: Jiangsu province • Highest ranked state-level ETDZ in Eastern China by CADZ in 2010
High-Tech Industrial Development Zone (HIDZ)	Specific areas aimed at commercializing research and development and encouraging specific industries including IT, electronics, pharmaceuticals, new materials, etc. Generally located next to universities These zones are generally quite similar to ETDZs but benefit from additional incentives for innovation	Kunshan New and Hi-Tech Industrial Development Zone (KSND) • Location: Jiangsu province • The first county level, state-approved zone in China
Free Trade Zone (FTZ)	Designated areas for export processing, international trade and bonded operations. They are also areas exempt from Chinese customs and enterprises in these areas can receive tax refunds on exports, imports and VAT	Waigaoqiao Free Trade Zone (WFTZ) • Location: Shanghai • China's oldest and largest Free Trade Zone
Export Processing Zone (EPZ)	Smaller-scale and simplified free trade zone, generally located within an existing development zone for the purpose of export processing. Generally subject to restrictive terms regarding manufactured goods for sale in local markets	Beihai Export Processing Zone • Location: Guangxi province • Nearest export processing zone to ASEAN countries
Bonded Logistics Zone	Areas where specific logistic activities can be carried out, subject to unique customs taxes. Traditionally located near ports or airports to facilitate aggregation of shipments or assembly. Rents are generally higher and these areas are not intended for setting up of factories or manufacturing bases. Bonded logistics zones are also becoming increasingly common around China. For those who use this type of zone, they go through customs when entering the zone but do not need to do so again	Hangjiagang Bonded Logistics Zone • Location: Jiangsu province • One of largest logistics zones in China

- Annual turnover (RMB 100 billion+)
- Tax income
- Export volume
- FDI

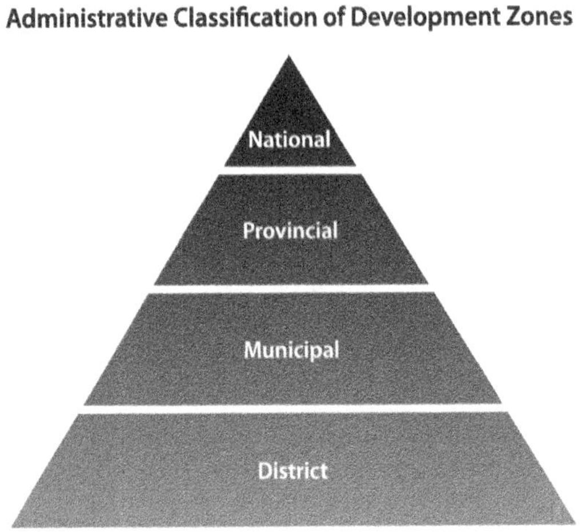

There are a number of benefits associated with choosing national versus provincial, municipal or district certified parks. The higher ranked the park, the greater degree of autonomy the managers have in approving projects and tenants. For current or potential tenants of the park, great autonomy generally means administrative tasks can be completed more quickly and inexpensively. Furthermore, higher-ranked zones also generally benefit from more support from the central government and more highly developed infrastructure. The major benefits associated with choosing a lower ranked park are typically related to lower land costs.

Keep in mind that larger and more established zones are not always better. Smaller companies operating in a national zone may find they do not receive all the same incentives larger corporations in the same area will receive. Similarly, resource availability and management capability vary greatly among zones and in fact, a district-level development zone may offer more incentives to smaller projects than a larger zone might.

3.10 Benefits of Locating in Development Zones

There are a large number of benefits associated with development zones and these areas are attractive draws for investors looking for an easier way to take advantage of Chinese labor and other inputs.

- *Preferential policies compared to non-development zone areas*
  Development zones receive a number of regulatory benefits and privileges aimed at reducing the cost of investment and facilitating importing and exporting.

Specifically, benefits include lowered land costs, tax awards and exemptions, facilitated customs clearance and ease of access to domestic markets. In particular where taxes are concerned, some higher-ranked zones (i.e. national zones) have the ability to provide certain exemptions from national taxes.

> When choosing a development zone, the first thing I would ask is 'Who else is already there?' If there are reasonable companies and businesses there, from a similar background as yours, who are having a good experience—it's much more likely your company will have a positive experience.
> —Michael Cole, Managing Director, Rightsite.asia

- *Support and participation of government*
  The government's support of development zones, at multiple levels, means foreign investors receive support in different terms and scopes. First, eager to attract foreign investors and consequentially boost the area's employment and economic wealth, zone management will often be quick to respond to changes in needs related to regulatory or market changes. Local governments can also provide accounting, legal, marketing and consulting services to help investors. The central government's willingness to aid in the growth of these areas has manifested itself in the form of an improved policy framework and consequentially, clearer legal and regulatory standards.
- *Autonomy*
  Development zones are granted a high degree of autonomy, although many are government-sponsored projects which are run by state-owned enterprises. Many zones have the ability to unilaterally make decisions regarding investment projects and potential clients, which expedites regulatory and administrative tasks in the favor of investors.
- *Resource availability*
  Zones which specialize in certain industries/sectors will likely have access to specific resources and expertise which are favorable for investors.
- *Hubs of technology, learning and innovation*
  Development zones are often hubs for creativity and innovation, stemming from the provision of government incentives, competition between tenants and the presence of highly skilled labor.

3.11 Factors to Consider when Choosing a Zone

Above all, the right type of development zone for an investor will depend on their specific business needs—industry, import/export plans, location of suppliers, labor/land/power requirements, scale of operations, etc. The factors which draw one investor to a particular development zone and another investor elsewhere are generally unique to the investor. So the first step to development zone selection is a self-evaluation of your company's priorities.

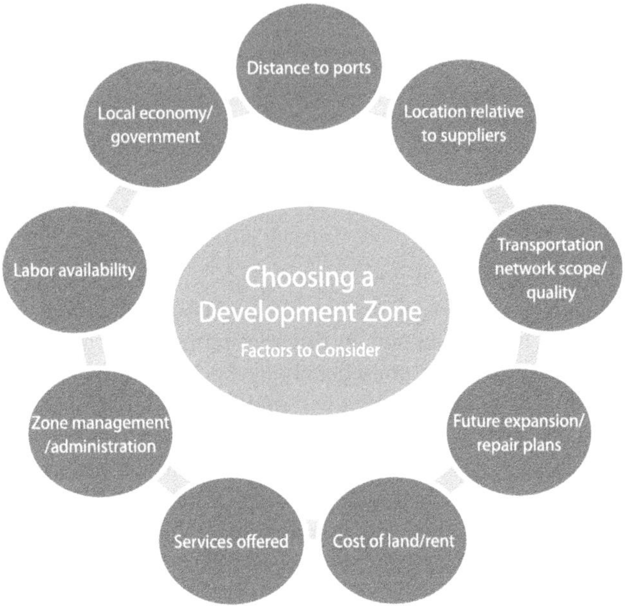

Once you've established these priorities, work with a consultancy firm to narrow down a list of zones. In any location of interest, seek out a list of companies that are already located in that zone. If you find the zone is occupied by companies with a similar background as yours, in terms of country or region of origin and what line of business they are in, it is valuable to reach out and gauge what their experience has been like.

When narrowing down a list of sites, recruit professional assistance. Typically, due diligence in this field requires assessment of the site itself, and the legal and tax implications of locating there.

Be mindful of the zone's management and administrative practices. A well-run zone will be up to date on changes in regulations or in the marketplace which will affect you and will be able/willing to help you make the necessary adjustments.

Investigate the quality and scope of infrastructure networks; do not take statements about location lightly. High quality infrastructure will increase efficiency and lower transportation costs significantly. Keep a future-focused mindset and take plans for expansion or repair of these networks into account.

Finally, be conscious of the sustainability and future viability a zone. Regional governments are often extremely eager to set aside land for the future development of these areas. An excess supply of development zones in the 1990s and early 2000s left large areas of land idle and millions in invested infrastructure wasted.

The central government eventually stepped in and forced the closure of 77.2% of existing zones, decreasing the number from 6,866 in 2003 to 1,568 in 2006. Another intervention by the central government is neither impossible nor unlikely if growth of development zones blossoms out of control again in the future.

While the 2008 Tax Reform limited tax breaks and such incentives, such fantastic deals are all relatively temporary any way. At the end of the day, the reforms are advantageous to investors—no one wants to be in a zone that's going to go under and zones were competing to offer bigger and bigger breaks, to the point where it wasn't sustainable.

Now zones are realizing that they have to offer other selling points: better service, a higher level of professionalism, a better product, infrastructure, etc.
—Michael Cole, Managing Director, Rightsite.asia

When narrowing down a list of sites, recruit professional assistance. Typically, due diligence in this field requires assessment of the site itself, and the legal and tax implications of locating there.

3.12 Future Outlook

In 2008, the National People's Congress passed a new law ("Enterprise Income Tax Law of People's Republic of China") unifying the tax code and eliminating some of the tax advantages foreign companies in China had enjoyed. There was some concern that the changes to the corporate income tax rate would deter foreign investment in development zones.

Historically, foreign companies faced the same statutory tax rates as domestic companies but benefited from tax treatments, like reduced filing fees and preferential timelines. What this amounted to was a reduced real income tax rate for foreign companies. The new unified corporate income tax (CIT) is 25% and the new tax system was to be phased in over 5 years beginning in 2008 and the full effects should be realized by 2013. China joined the WTO in 2001 and the elimination of the former dual-track taxation system represents another step the country is taking to meet global business practices. In one respect, this implies a degree of security for investors, since the country can now be increasingly held to international standards and uncertainties in the regulatory environment begin to fade. This shift in development zones also parallels a larger, up and coming change in the Chinese economy as it continues to climb the global value chain towards more value-adding industries.

Despite its immediate affects, these changes in taxes could have a positive impact on development zones. The tax reform effectively forces zones to look at other ways to market themselves and other dimensions by which they might be differentiated. In the near future, investors will see zones shift their focus in a service-oriented direction as they look for new ways to attract investors.

Development zones will increasingly be required to offer value to their investors as opposed to only cost savings.

Development zones will also have to adjust to meet the challenges facing all China investors, including the increasingly important issue of labor recruitment. Development zones are responding to the labor recruitment challenge with agility, creating and marketing new communities with an attractive quality of life. For middle and high level management recruitment, labor recruitment is also being eased slightly by the development of high speed rail lines.

3.13 Additional Resources

CADZ
http://www.cadz.org.cn/en/
A resource which provides information on development zones, originally approved by the Ministry of Civil Affairs of the People's Republic of China. (Available in English and Chinese)

RightSite
http://rightsite.asia/index.php
Data and articles on specific parks and zones, as well as discussions relevant to industrial property owners. (Available in English and Chinese)

The World Bank
Building Engines for Growth and Competitiveness in China: Experiences with Special Economic Zones and Industrial Clusters by Douglas Zhihua Zeng

Major development zones in the Yangtze River Delta

Location	Government jurisdiction level	Name	Industry focus	Contact (Tel/Email/Website)
Shanghai				
Shanghai	National	Shanghai Hongqiao Economic and Technological Development Zone	International trading, consultation, general business	Tel: +86-21-6275-6888 Email: shudc@public1.sta.net.cn website: www.shade.com/main/
		Shanghai Minhang Economic and Technological Development Zone	Food and beverages, Pharmaceuticals, machine parts and equipment	Tel: +86-21-6430-0888, Email: smudc@online. sh.cn, succ@sh163.net website: www.smudc com/en/ index.htm
		Shanghai Waigaoqiao Free Trade Zone	International trading, warehousing and logistics, export processing	Tel: +86-21-5869-8500 Email: wgq@shwgq.com; http:// www.waigaoqiao.gov.cn http://www.shwgq.com
		Shanghai Jinqiao Export Processing Zone	IT and components, automobiles and parts, pharmaceuticals, electronic appliances	Tel: +86-21-5899-1818 Email: jqepz@public1.sta.net.cn Website: www.jinqiao.gov.cn
	Provincial	Lingang Industrial Park	Automobiles and parts, software, electronics, industrial equipment production, international trade	Tel: +86-21-68283222 Website: www.lgxc.gov.cn
		Shanghai Baoshan Industrial Zone	Steel processing, automated manufacturing, ship components, cargo transportation	Tel: +86-21-33851044 http://www.sbiz.gov.cn/
		Shanghai Chemical Industry Park	Natural gas, petrochemicals, fine chemicals, polymers and macromolecular materials	Tel: +86-21-6712-0000 Email: business.scip.com.cn Website: www.scip.com.cn/en
		Shanghai Jiading Industrial Zone	Auto parts, optical electronics, environmentally-friendly technology	Tel: +86-21-3996-6500 (Office), +86-021-3996-6552 Email: 005@ jdiz.com http://www.jdiz.com

(continued)

(continued)

Location	Government jurisdiction level	Name	Industry focus	Contact (Tel/Email/Website)
Shanghai				
Jiangsu				
Changzhou	National	Changzhou National High-Tech Zone	General electronics, optical electronics, pharmaceuticals, fine chemicals	Tel: +86-519-8510-7129, 8512-7096 Email: Jzhou@ cznd.org.cn, lxxia@cznd.org. cn http://www.cznd.com
	Provincial	Qishuyan Economic Development Zone	Textiles, automobile Parts, food and beverages	Tel: +86-519-88401579 http://www.qedz.gov.cn
		Wujin Hi-Tech Industrial Zone	General electronics, machine parts and equipment, auto parts, general trading, warehousing and logistics	Tel: +86-0519-8622-0089, 8622-0100, 8622-0091, 8622-0092, 8622-0093 http://www.wujinzone.org
		Liyang Economic Development Zone	Telecommunications equipment, fine chemicals, automobiles and parts, pharmaceuticals, medical equipment, research and development, heavy industry	Tel: +86-519-8730-1133, +86-519-8731-2802 Email: cisc@ lyedz.cn, Invest-liyang@163. com http://www.lyedz.cn
Nanjing	National	Nanjing Economic and Technical Development Zone	IT and components, pharmaceuticals, fine chemicals, polymers and macromolecular materials	Tel: +86-25-5800800 Email: gwh@ njxg.com http://www.njxg.com
		Nanjing New and Hi-Tech Industrial Development Zone	IT and components, pharmaceuticals, polymers and macromolecular materials	Tel: +86-25-5884-3666 Email: njgx@njnhz.gov.cn http://www.njnhz.gov.cn
	Provincial	Nanjing Jiangning Economic Technological Development Zone	Automobiles and parts, food and beverage, electronics, research and development	Tel: +86-25-5211-0888 http://www.jndz.gov.cn

(continued)

(continued)

Location	Government jurisdiction level	Name	Industry focus	Contact (Tel/Email/Website)
Shanghai				
Suzhou	National	China–Singapore Suzhou Industrial Park	Electronics, machine parts and equipment, pharmaceuticals, fine chemicals, precision Engineering, Polymers and macromolecular materials	Tel: + 86-512-6668-1535 Email: jsx@sipac.gov.cn http://www.sipac.gov.cn
		Suzhou National New and Hi-Tech Development Zone	Automobiles, pharmaceuticals, construction materials, fine chemicals, software, electronics, raw material processing, research and development, general trading	Tel: +86-512-6825-1888 Email: snd@snd.gov.cn http://www.snd.gov.cn
Taizhou	National	Taizhou Pharmaceutical Hi-Tech Industry Park	Pharmaceuticals, medical equipment	Tel: +86-523-8682-0000, 8620-0001
	Provincial	Taixing Economic Development Zone	Electronics, textiles, fine chemicals, software, general trading, pharmaceuticals,Industrial equipment, raw material processing	Tel: +86-523-8760-7118 http://www.txedz.com
Wuxi	National	Wuxi New District	Electronics, IT components, general/optical electronics	Tel: +86-0510-8521-7388 Email: invest@wnd.gov.cn http://www.wnd.gov.cn
Yangzhou	National	Yangzhou Economic Development Zone	Automobiles and parts, raw material processing, telecommunications equipment	Tel: +86-514-8796-2926 (Mr Xiansheng Ji) http://www.zgyzedz.gov.cn
Zhejiang				
Hangzhou	National	Hangzhou Economic and Technological Development Area	IT components, machine parts, food and beverages	Tel: +86-571-86912057 Email: invest@heda.gov.cn http://www.heda.gov.cn
Jiashan	Provincial	Jiashan Economic Development Zone	Electronics, textiles, industrial/telecom equipment	Tel: +86-5734183868 Email: Kfqif@public.js.jxptt.zj.cn http://www.jsedz.com
Jiaxing	National	Jiaxing Port Economic Development Zone	Automobiles and parts, food and beverages, textiles, heavy industry, R&D	Tel: +86-573-85527003 Email: gwj@gw.jiaxing.cn http://www.eastport.com.cn

(continued)

(continued)

Location	Government jurisdiction level	Name	Industry focus	Contact (Tel/Email/Website)
Shanghai				
Ningbo	National	Ningbo Economic and Technological Development Zone	Automobiles and parts, textiles, heavy industry, industrial/medical/telecom equipment, raw material processing, R&D, crafts and toys	Tel: +86-574-86850225 Email: webmaster@netd.com.cn, ganyf@netd.gov.cn http://www.netd.gov.cn
Pinghu	National	National Jiaxing Export Processing Zone	Machinery, electronics, publishing, packaging, general trading	Tel: +86-573-85588108 Email: zdl666@vip.sina.com
	Provincial	Pinghu Economic Development Zone	Telecommunications equipment, IT components, optical electronics, microelectronics	Tel: +86-5735099009 Email: pedz@mail.jxptt.zj.cn phdz@pinghu.com; http://www.pinghu.com
		Zhapu Economic Development Zone	Electronics, telecom/industrial equipment, construction materials, automobile Parts, R&D, general trading	Tel: +86-573-85581090 http://www.zhapu.gov.cn

Appendix, Directory, References

Shanghai

Government

Shanghai Government www.shanghai.gov.cn	Shanghai Economy Commission www.shec.gov.cn	Shanghai Investment www.shanghaiinvest.com/cn/index
Shanghai Statistics Information www.stats-sh.gov.cn	Shanghai FDI Promotion www.investment.gov.cn	Shanghai Commerce www.commerce.sh.cn
Shanghai Government Procurement http://www.shzfcg.gov.cn:8090/new_web/zfcg_new.jsp	Shanghai Small and Medium-sized Enterprises www.sse.gov.cn	Shanghai Foreign Affairs Office www.shfao.gov.cn
Shanghai Administration of Industry and Commerce www.sgs.gov.cn	Shanghai Development and Reform Commission www.shdpc.gov.cn	Shanghai Overseas Chinese Affairs Office www.overseas.sh.cn
News		
Shanghai Daily www.Shanghaidaily.com	Xinmin Evening News www.xmwb.com.cn	Shanghai Stocks Exchange www.sse.com.cn/sseportal/ps/zhs/home.html
Eastday.com English english.eastday.com	Xinmin Weekly www.xinminweekly.com.cn	Sina Shanghai Channel www.sh.sina.com.cn
Shanghai Media Group www.smg.cn	Shanghai Online www.online.sh.cn	China News Shanghai Channel www.sh.chinanews.com.cn
Wenhui Xinmin Press Group www.news365.com.cn	Shanghai Tourism Site www.shanghaitour.net	Xinhua Net Shanghai Channel www.sh.xinhua.org
Expatriate life		
City Weekend—Shanghai www.cityweekend.com.cn/shanghai	Shanghai Expat www.shanghaiexpat.com	Shanghai Talk www.talkmagazines.cn
That's Shanghai www.urbanatomy.com	Shanghaiist www.shanghaiist.com	SH Magazine www.shmag.cn
Major consulates		
Argentina www.consuargensh.com	Cuba www.conscuba.cn	India www.indianconsulate.org.cn/site/

(continued)

Dezan Shira & Associates et al. (eds.), *The Yangtze River Delta*, China Briefing,
DOI: 10.1007/978-3-642-27624-8, © Asia Briefing Ltd. 2012

(continued)

Australia
www.aus-in-shanghai.com

Austria
www.bmeia.gv.at/cn/botschaft/peking.html

Belgium
www.diplobel.org/shanghai

Brazil
http://www.baxi.org.cn/index_cn.htm

Canada
www.shanghai.gc.ca

Mexico
http://www.consulmex-shanghai.com/

Monaco
http://moroccoembassy.cn/

Netherlands
www.cgshanghai.org

New Zealand
www.cgshanghai.org

Norway
www.norway.org.cn/

Pakistan
www.pakconsulateshanghai.org.cn

Philippines
www.philcongenshanghai.org/cnweb2009/index.htm

Czech Republic
www.mzv.cz/beijing

Denmark
www.denmark.cn/shanghai

Finland
www.finland.cn/public/default.aspx?culture=zh-CN&contentlan=20

France
www.consulfrance-shanghai.org

Germany
www.schanghai.diplo.de/Vertretung/shanghai/zh/Startseite.html

Poland
www.polandshanghai.com

Romania
beijing.mae.ro/index.php?lang=cn&id=66004

Russia
www.russia.org.cn/chn/

Serbia and Montenegro
www.scgshanghai.com

Singapore
www.gov.sg/mfa/shanghai

South Africa
dhashanghai@hotpop.com

South Korea
http://china.koreanembassy.cn

Ireland
embassyofireland.cn/Ireland-Chinese/index.htm

Israel
www.shanghai.mfa.gov.il

Italy
www.italyvac.cn/

Japan
www.shanghai.cn.emb-japan.go.jp/cn/index_cn.htm

Malaysia
www.matrade.gov.cn

Spain
www.embassyofspain.cn/cn/index.htm

Sweden
www.swedenabroad/shanghai

Switzerland
www.switzerland.com.cn

Thailand
http://www.thaishanghai.com/th/index.php

Turkey
www.turkey.org.cn/cn/emmain.asp

United Kingdom
www.uk.cn

United States of America
www.usembassy-china.org.cn/shanghai

Major business associations

American Chamber of Commerce
www.amcham-shanghai.org

Australian Chamber of Commerce
www.austchamshanghai.com

Benelux Business Association
www.bbash.com

British Chamber of Commerce
www.sha.britcham.org

Canada Chamber of Commerce
http://www.cancham.asia/

Canada China Business Council
www.ccbc.com

Canadian Business Forum
http://canada.businessforumnews.com/

China Link, Liverpool Chamber of Commerce
www.chinalink.org.uk

China-Italy Chamber of Commerce
www.cameraitacina.com

Danish Business Association of Shanghai
www.dccc.com.cn

Direct Marketing Association
www.thechinadma.com

EU Chamber of Commerce
www.euccc.com.cn

Enterprise Ireland
http://www.enterprise-ireland.com/en/

Finland Trade Centre
http://www.finpro.fi/

HK Chamber of Commerce
http://www.hkccc.cn/

Confederation of Indian Industry
www.ciionline.org

Indonesia Business Association
www.indosnet.com

Japanese Club of Commerce and Industry
http://www.cjcci.biz/public_html/index_cn.html

Korean Chamber of Commerce
http://china.korcham.net/

Shanghai Singapore Business Association
www.ssba.org.cn

Swiss Chamber of Commerce
www.swisscenters.org

(continued)

(continued)

China Britain Business Council (CBBC)
www.cbbc.org

China Chamber on International Commerce
www.ccpit-shanghai.com

French Chamber of Commerce
www.ccifc.org

German Chamber of Commerce
http://china.ahk.de/membership/shanghai/

Exhibition Centers

Shanghai Everbright International
www.secec.com

Shanghai New International Exhibition Center
www.sniec.net

Shanghai International Convention Center
www.sicec.net

Shanghai International Exhibition Center (INTEX)
www.intex-sh.com

Shanghai Mart
www.shanghaimart.com

Business Centers

APBC—Shanghai—Platinum Xintiandi
233, Taicang Road
Tel: (21) 5175 7777
www.apbcoffices.com/

APBC—Shanghai—Times Square
26/F Shanghai Times Square Office Tower, 93 Huaihai Zhong Road
Tel: (21) 5117 9333
www.apbcoffices.com/

The Executive Centre—Chonghing Finance Centre
12/F Chonghing Finance Center.
288 Nanjing Road West
Tel: (21) 61337821
www.executivecentre.com

The Executive Centre—Citic Square
35/F, Citic Square,
1168 Nanjing Xi Road
Tel: (21) 5252 4618
www.executivecentre.com

The Executive Centre—Xintiandi
5/F 159 Madang Lu, Xintiandi
Tel: (21) 6135 7188
www.executivecentre.com

Lister—The Mansion
457 Shan Xi Road North Block 1
Tel: (21) 6141 8484
www.officelister.com

Lister—The Tower
14/F, Jinjiang Xiangyang Tower,
993 Nanjing West Road
Tel: (21) 6272 7899
www.officelister.com

Lister—Hongkong Plaza
26/F Hongkong Plaza, 283 Huaihai Zhong Lu
Tel: (21) 6103 5888
www.officelister.com

Apollo—Jingan Center
1440 Yan An Road (Central)
Tel: (21) 6133 1888
www.apollobizctr.com

Apollo—Tomson Center
22 Tomson Commercial Building,
710 Dong Fang Road, Pudong,
Tel: (21) 6165 2288
www.apollobizctr.com

Lister—The SOHO
Building #1 & #3, 128 Da Tian Road
Tel: (21) 6103 5888
www.officelister.com

Office General—Plaza 66 Tower I
1266 Nanjing Road West, 39/F
Tel: (21) 6288 3288
www.officegeneral.com

Office General—Plaza 66 Tower II
1366 Nanjing Road West, 15/F
Tel: (21) 6288 3288
www.officegeneral.com

Office General—OG Plaza
2601 Xietu Road Xuhui District
Tel: (21) (21) 6288 3288
www.officegeneral.com

Regus—Shanghai—Shui on Plaza
room 1201, Shui on Plaza, 333 Huaihai Zhong Road Tel: (21) 5116 0300
www.regus.cn

Regus—Shanghai—Bund Center
18/F, 222 Yan'an Dong Road
Tel: (21) 6335 2077
www.regus.cn

Apollo—XuJiaHui Center
16F Feidiao International Building,
1065 Zhao Jia Bang Road
Tel: (21) 5158 1688
www.apollobizctr.com

The Executive Centre—The Centre
20/F 989 Changle Road
Tel: (21) 5116 6888
www.executivecentre.com

Regus—Shanghai—Jin Mao Building
31/F Jin Mao Tower,
88 Century Avenue
Tel: (21) 2890 9983
www.regus.cn

Regus—Shanghai—One Corporate
15/F, building 1, no.22 Corporate Avenue
Tel: (21) 6122 1001
www.regus.cn

Regus—Shanghai—Oriental Center
18/F, 699 Nanjing Xi Road
Tel: (21) 5211 0805
www.regus.cn

Servcorp—Citigroup Tower
Level 23, Citigroup Tower
33 Huayuanshiqiao Road,
Shanghai Tel: (21) 6101 0000
www.servcorp.com

Servcorp—Shanghai Kerry Centre
Level 29, Shanghai Kerry Centre
No.1515, Nanjing West Road
Tel: (21) 6103 7000
www.servcorp.com

Servcorp—Somekh Building, Rockbund
5/F Somekh Building, Rockbund
No.149 Yuanmingyuan Road
Tel: (21) 3120 3000
www.servcorp.com

Jiangsu

Government

China Jiangsu
www.jschina.com.cn

China Jiangsu
www.jiangsu.gov.cn

China Jiangsu Tourism
www.jstour.com

China News.com Jiangsu Channel
www.js.chinanews.com.cn

Jiangsu Provincial Department of Culture
http://www.jscnt.gov.cn/

Jiangsu Radio and TV
www.jsgd.com.cn

Jiangsu Statistic Bureau
www.jssb.gov.cn

Jiangsu Small and Medium-sized Enterprises
www.jste.gov.cn

Jiangsu Economic and Information Technology Commission
www.jsetc.gov.cn

Jiangsu Development and Reform Commission
www.jsdpc.gov.cn

Jiangsu Government Procurement Office
http://www.ccgp-jiangsu.gov.cn/pub/jszfcg/index.html.

Jiangsu Economic Information Network
www.js.cei.gov.cn

Jiangsu Overseas Chinese
www.jsqw.com

News

Xinhua Net Jiangsu Channel
www.js.xinhuanet.com

Jiangsu Commercial News
www.njnews.cn/jssb/index.htm
Business associations

Jiangsu Association for International Exchange of Personnel
http://jiangsu.caiep.org/

Yangtze Economic News
www.yangtse.com

Zhejiang

Government

Zhejiang Government Site
www.zhejiang.gov.cn

Zhejiang Economic Information
www.zei.gov.cn

Zhejiang Logistics
www.zj56.com.cn

Zhejiang Small and Medium-sized Enterprises
www.zjsme.gov.cn

Zhejiang Provincial Bureau of Statistics
www.zj.stats.gov.cn

Zhejiang Economy and Trade Committee
www.zjjmw.gov.cn

Zhejiang Federation of Industry and Commerce
www.zjfic.org.cn

Zhejiang Administration of Industry and Commerce
www.zjaic.gov.cn

Zhejiang Provincial Development and Reform Commission
www.zjdpc.gov.cn

Department of Commerce of Zhejiang
www.zcom.gov.cn

Zhejiang Overseas Chinese
www.zjqb.com/home.do

(continued)

(continued)

News

Zhejiang Online
www.zjol.com.cn

Zhejiang News
www.news.zj.com/zhejiang

Zhejiang City Life
www.zj.com

Zhejiang Daily
http://zjdaily.zjol.com.cn/html/2011-08/17/node_18.htm

Zhejiang TV
www.cztv.com.cn

Xinhua Net Zhejiang Channel
www.zj.xinhuanet.com

Quzhou Daily
http://www.qz828.com/

Taichou Daily
http://paper.taizhou.com.cn/

Jiangxin Daily
http://www.cnjxol.com/

Jinhua Daily
http://www.jhnews.com.cn/

Yiwu Business News
www.ywnews.cn

Shangyu Daily
http://www.shangyuribao.cn/

Xiaoshan Daily
http://xsnet.cn/

Zhuji Daily
www.zjrb.cn

Business associations

Zhejiang Association of Certified Accoutant
www.zicpa.org.cn

Zhejiang Software Industry Association
www.zsia.org

Zhejiang Restaurants Association
www.zjhotels.org

Zhejiang International Talents Exchange Association
http://zhejiang.caiep.org/

China Council for the Promotion of International Trade Zhejiang Sub-cuncil
http://www.ccpitzj.gov.cn/index_E.php

Anhui

Government

Anhui Investment Promotion
www.ahinvest.gov.cn

China Anhui Import Export Commodities
http://www.ahexporter.com/

Anhui Association of Enterprises with Foreign Investment
www.ahws.com.cn

Anhui Economic and Information TechnologyCommission
www.aheic.gov.cn

Anhui Communication Administration
www.ahta.gov.cn/ais

Anhui Development and Reform Commission
www.ahpc.gov.cn

The Bureau of Commerce of Anhui Province
www.ahbofcom.gov.cn

Anhui Administration of Industry and Commerce
www.ahaic.gov.cn

Anhui State Administration of Taxation
www.ah-n-tax.gov.cn

Anhui Government Procurement
www.ccgp-anhui.gov.cn

Anhui Administrative Service Center
www.ahzw.gov.cn

Anhui Small and Medium- Sized Enterprises
www.smeah.gov.cn

News

Anhui News Portal
www.anhuinews.com

Anhui Hotline
www.ah163.net

People's Daily Anhui Branch
ah.people.com.cn

Anhui Radio
www.ahradio.com.cn

China News Anhui Channel
www.ah.chinanews.com.cn

Anhui TV
www.ahtv.cn

Xinhua Net Anhui Channel
www.ah.xinhuanet.com

Anhui Market Newspaper
www.ahscb.com

(continued)

(continued)

Major Business Associations

Anhui Software Industry Association
www.ahsoft.org.cn

Anhui Bureau of Foreign Experts Affairs / Anhui Association for International Exchange of Personnel
www.anhui.caiep.org

Anhui Hotels Association
www.ahfdy.com

Anhui E-Commerce Association
www.aheca.org.cn

Anhui Vendors Association
www.ahghs.com

International Anhui Business People
www.huishangnet.com

Glossary

Term	Meaning
AIC	Administration of Industry and Commerce
BOFTEC	Bureau of Foreign Trade and Economic Cooperation (local approvals authority)
CIT	Corporate Income tax
CJV	Cooperative (Contractual) Joint Venture
EPZ	Export Processing Zone (state-level)
EJV	Equity Joint Venture
ETDZ	Economic and Technological Development Zone (state-level)
FDI	Foreign Direct Investment
FICE	Foreign Invested Commercial Enterprise
FIE	Foreign Invested Enterprise
FTZ	Free Trade Zone (state-level)
HIDZ	High-Tech Industrial Development Zone (state-level)
IIT	Individual Income Tax
JV	Joint Venture
M&A	Merger and Acquisition
MOC	Ministry of Commerce
MOF	Ministry of Finance
NDRC	National Development and Reform Commission
PRC	People's Republic of China
RMB	Renminbi (Chinese currency unit, also know as Yuan)
RO	Representative Office
SAFE	State Administration of Foreign Exchange
SAIC	State Administration of Industry and Commerce
SAT	State Administration of Taxation
SDPC	State Development and Planning Commission
SETC	State Economic and Trade Commission
SEZ	Special Economic Zone (state-level)
VAT	Value Added Tax
WFOE	Wholly Foreign-Owned Enterprise
WTO	World Trade Organization

Dezan Shira & Associates et al. (eds.), *The Yangtze River Delta*, China Briefing,
DOI: 10.1007/978-3-642-27624-8, © Asia Briefing Ltd. 2012

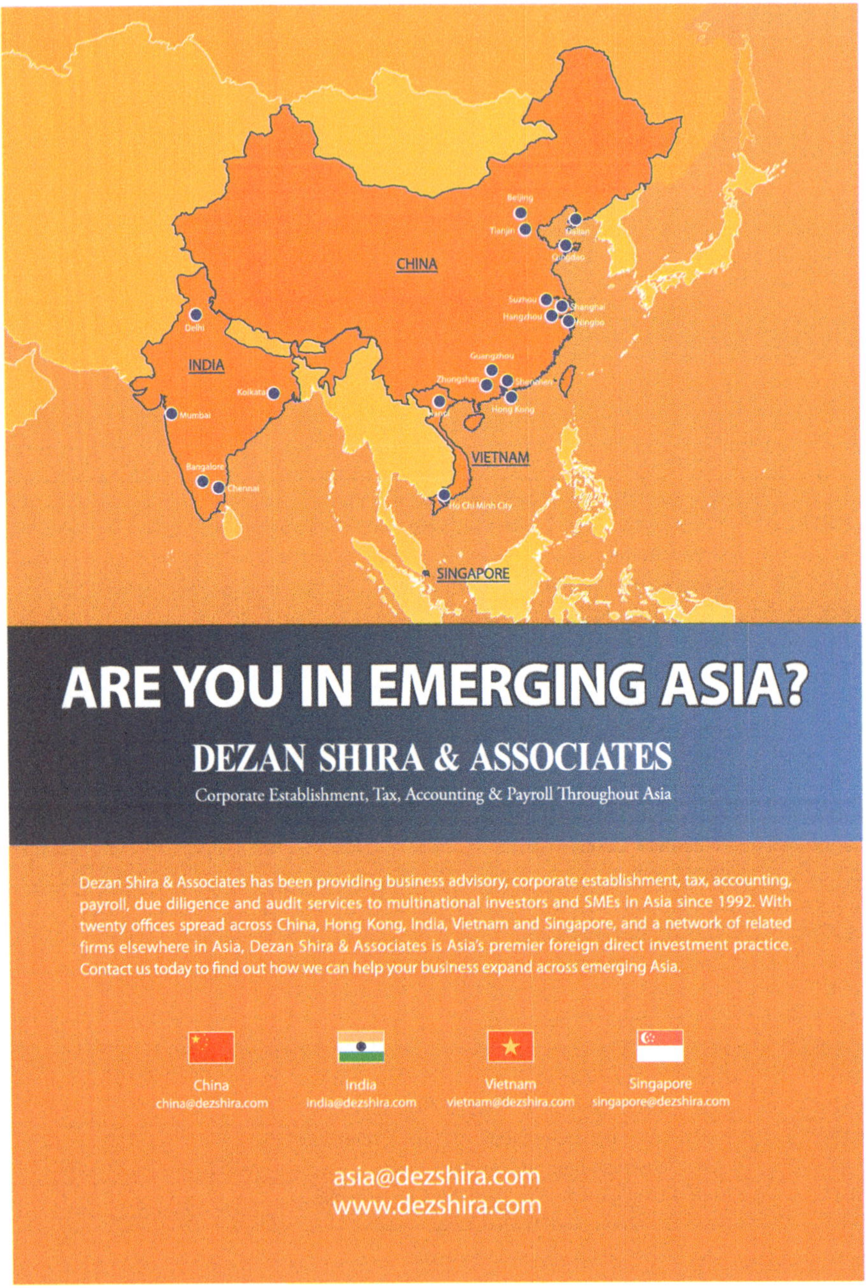
CHINA
Beijing
Tianjin
Dalian
Qingdao
Suzhou
Shanghai
Hangzhou
Ningbo
Guangzhou
Zhongshan
Shenzhen
Hong Kong
Hanoi
INDIA
Delhi
Kolkata
Mumbai
Bangalore
Chennai
VIETNAM
Ho Chi Minh City
SINGAPORE
ARE YOU IN EMERGING ASIA?
DEZAN SHIRA & ASSOCIATES
Corporate Establishment, Tax, Accounting & Payroll Throughout Asia
Dezan Shira & Associates has been providing business advisory, corporate establishment, tax, accounting, payroll, due diligence and audit services to multinational investors and SMEs in Asia since 1992. With twenty offices spread across China, Hong Kong, India, Vietnam and Singapore, and a network of related firms elsewhere in Asia, Dezan Shira & Associates is Asia's premier foreign direct investment practice. Contact us today to find out how we can help your business expand across emerging Asia.
China
china@dezshira.com
India
india@dezshira.com
Vietnam
vietnam@dezshira.com
Singapore
singapore@dezshira.com
asia@dezshira.com
www.dezshira.com

ASIA BRIEFING

TECHNICAL & REGIONAL BUSINESS GUIDES

China Briefing produces a highly-regarded series of technical and regional business guides, including:

Download All Titles from The Asia Briefing Bookstore

www.asiabriefingmedia.com

ASIA BRIEFING

Regional Business Intelligence

From the Asia Foreign Direct Investment Practice
Dezan Shira & Associates

www.asiabriefingmedia.com

CHINA BRIEFING
www.china-briefing.com

INDIA BRIEFING
www.india-briefing.com

RUSSIA BRIEFING
www.russia-briefing.com

MONGOLIA BRIEFING
www.mongolia-briefing.com

VIETNAM BRIEFING
www.vietnam-briefing.com

2point6billion.com
www.2point6billion.com

DEZAN SHIRA & ASSOCIATES

Business Advisory · Corporate Establishment · Tax · Accounting · Payroll · Due Diligence · Audit

CHINA INDIA VIETNAM SINGAPORE

www.dezshira.com

The manufacturer's authorised representative in the EU is Springer Nature Customer Service Centre GmbH, Europaplatz 3, 69115 Heidelberg, Germany. If you have any concerns regarding our products, please contact ProductSafety@springernature.com

Printed and bound by CPI Group (UK) Ltd, Croydon, CR0 4YY
30/09/2026
02225575-0012